T0369690

TASTE AS EXPERIENCE

Arts and Traditions of the Table

ARTS AND TRADITIONS OF THE TABLE:
PERSPECTIVES ON CULINARY HISTORY

ALBERT SONNENFELD, SERIES EDITOR

For a complete list of books in the series, see pages 157–58.

TASTE AS EXPERIENCE

THE PHILOSOPHY AND AESTHETICS OF FOOD

Nicola Perullo

COLUMBIA UNIVERSITY PRESS   NEW YORK

COLUMBIA UNIVERSITY PRESS

Publishers Since 1893

New York   Chichester, West Sussex

Copyright © 2016 Columbia University Press

Italian edition: *Il Gusto come esperienza,* copyright © 2012 Slow Food Editore S.r.l.

Via della Mendicità Istruita, 45–12042 Bra (Cn) Italy

Phone: +39 0172 419611; Fax +39 0172 411218

editorinfo@slowfood.it—www.slowfood.it—www.giunti.it

Library of Congress Cataloging-in-Publication Data

Perullo, Nicola, 1970-

[Gusto come esperienza. English]

Taste as experience : the philosophy and aesthetics of food /

Nicola Perullo. — American edition.

pages cm. — (Arts and traditions of the table)

Translation of: Il gusto come esperienza. Bra, 2012.

Includes bibliographical references and index.

ISBN 978-0-231-17348-3 (cloth)

1. Gastronomy. 2. Taste. I. Title.

TX641.P47313 2016

641.01'3—dc23

2015024701

Cover design: Mary Ann Smith

Cover image: © Pando Hall/Getty

CONTENTS

Preface to the American Edition   vii
Foreword by Massimo Montanari   xiii

INTRODUCTION   1
The Project   1
Difficulties and Resistances   14
Possibilities and Perspectives   21

FIRST MODE OF ACCESS: PLEASURE   27
Pleasure, Enjoyment, and Intelligence   29
Pleasure, Image, and Pathology   35
Criticism and the Look of Childhood   38
Pleasure as Nature in Culture   43
The Ethics of Pleasure: Good That Does "Good"   48

SECOND MODE OF ACCESS: KNOWLEDGE   53
Learning About Quality, Cultivating Taste   54
Tasting the World   60
Dressed Taste, Image, and Representation   66
Taste, Conflicts, and Culture   70
Curiosity, Expertise, Criticism (with Risks Included)   74
Taste and Sustainability: The Good That Grounds the Good   83
Taste and Diet   86

THIRD MODE OF ACCESS: INDIFFERENCE   89
Essen Non Est Percipi   91
Contingent Indifference   97
Compulsive Indifference and Atmospheric Indifference   101
The Neutral   106
The Extension of Pleasure and the Limits
of Gustatory Exclusivism   111

THE WISDOM OF TASTE,
THE TASTE OF WISDOM   115
Taste and Pleasure, Experience, and Wisdom   116
Wise Expertise (Epicurus, Hume, and Dewey)   120
Regulation Without Rules   124
Flexibility: The Forest and the Coast   128
Conviviality: Discord and Gustatory Empathy   131
Take My Advice   132

Notes   137
References   139
Index   147

PREFACE TO THE AMERICAN EDITION

WHEN GOOD IS THE WISDOM OF TASTE: THREE STEPS TO A BETTER PERCEPTION IN EXPERIENCING FOOD

To demonstrate how honored and pleased I am to have this book translated into English for the American edition, I would like to briefly depict the motivation that generated it. This essay is the result of the intertwining of my theoretical reflection as a philosopher and my practical experience as a food and wine lover over the past twenty years. My initial interest in wine and food at the beginning of the 1990s was by chance, and only after a certain number of years was my expertise directed toward a theoretical path. Nevertheless, the theorizing that you will find in these pages is heterodox and not systematic. In fact, I have always found the valorization of food that doesn't take into account its experiential, narrative, and practical dimension to be paradoxical. Today this paradox looms large: there are numerous conventions, in many disciplines or cross-disciplines, on the importance of taste and gastronomy in which care is not taken to organize good convivial settings, to eat good food or drink good wine. Indeed, in some cases, there is only speaking and no eating. Either one speaks or one eats: this *aut aut* expresses a dichotomous and hierarchizing point of view on which much of our culture is based. Instead, the convivial experience proposes a different perspective in which real eating and metaphorical eating intertwine.

In effect, in the humanities and in philosophy there are different ways of approaching food as a theme of study, but I believe that increasing interest in this matter has been driven mainly by two different strategies. The first one can be called the "rising strategy": food is important because *it is* Culture with capital C, that which is also called "high" culture in contrast to "simple" and "material" culture. This strategy has already been clearly expanded today. The second strategy, on the other hand, can be named the "lowering strategy": food is important because all culture *is* food, in both the physical and the metaphorical sense. Or rather, beyond the opposition between the physical and the metaphorical. To state this, we need to see culture and knowledge differently, of course, and to deconstruct some stabile dichotomies and hierarchies. This essay follows this second strategy. In other words, my attempt has been to make philosophy *with* food rather than *of* food, stemming from a particular and heterodox phenomenological perspective. I would call it a phenomenology "from inside" since I attempted to describe the tasting experience by taking into account the active perspective of the participant more than that of the observer. This choice is due to my conviction that a philosophy of food, to the extent that it is a philosophy *with* food, depends on a transformational interrogation and not only on a descriptive one. Food is not only an object for reflection, but also a matter that affects reflection. The experience of food is specific perception: a direct relationship, a unique piece of the external solid world that we incorporate into ourselves. This suggests important assumptions and consequences for the way we think. *Taste as Experience* is therefore an attempt to approach food not as an object of study among others, but rather as a matter of a specific system that requires a specific narrative.

This essay is constructed around the concept of taste. Rooted in common sense, as has been frequently observed, is the idea that there is no possible way of constructively discussing what is good, in terms of *that which is pleasing to taste*. Discussions regarding goodness are often taken for granted and contained within the boundary of the seemingly obvious question of so-called subjectivity and objectivity. The problem of taste is the problem of the subject. More precisely, it is

the problem of subjectivity in individual consciousness and awareness of identity. However, this definition has a history. The concept
of taste as an individual response, in terms of pleasure and knowledge, sensorially external (visual, auditory, or, in the case of food,
taste/olfactory), is not, in fact, a very old one. It was born within the
context of modernity, in which a new paradigm of consciousness was
defined that determined the concept of something akin to *subjectivity*.
This goes together with the idea that *outside* there is a world made up
of objects. Taste then becomes a measure for recognizing quality and
expressing values: the beautiful and the ugly, the good and the bad.
Much of modern thought has proposed various solutions to guarantee that taste, as so defined, has its own legitimacy. Immanuel Kant,
for example, wants to separate taste in the metaphorical sense, the
taste for beauty, from physical taste, that of the palate. According to
Kant, only the taste for beauty can be shared and therefore universal,
not that of the palate since it does not allow for objectivity. The fact
that we assimilate and incorporate external material brings about
an extreme *individualization* of the perceptual experience, undermin-
ing its universal value. The question that arises in this essay is then:
can we deconstruct this paradigm, which has become more or less
established, and promote a different scenario that is both positive
and useful? I suggest three steps that the reader will find through the
chapters of the book.

First step: Show the complexity of taste by claiming *expertise* (especially *know-how*, competence). It is obvious that taste can be examined
by separating out the collective shared recognition of quality from
that of individual pleasure. The saying goes that there's no account-
ing for (discussing) taste, but discussions regarding taste are very
frequent and this has a meaning. Taste does not only refer to the
pleasure an individual experiences when eating, but also the recognition of the quality of what is eaten. The difference between pleasure
and the recognition of quality depends on the capacity of the consumer: in gastronomy, it is through the acquisition of a certain *expertise* that it becomes possible to distinguish "I like" as an expression
of preference from "good" as a judgment of quality. *Expertise* plays an
important role: whoever is unable to distinguish the two will not be

able to notice the difference between pleasure and goodness. However, those who can will be able to discuss the quality of a food even without liking it personally. *Expertise*, therefore, allows us to take an important first step toward understanding the meaning of "good" in a social and historical sense. "Good" is not just what I like, but rather a cultural and negotiated value. Lévi-Strauss identified it as the relationship between "good to eat" and "good to think about," which is the key factor for understanding models of taste: what's good to eat is that which is good to think about. The great anthropologist gave a primary and fundamental role to ethics in valuing what is "good" with reference to taste.

Second step: The return to having a look at taste "from below" since everyone eats. The idea that "taste is culture" is an important achievement, but it still doesn't explain everything. What does it mean to be an expert—or a cultured person—in a domain that is immersed by its nature in everyday life? This perceptive peculiarity of our relationship to food consists in always experiencing an *interested assimilation*. Because the specifics of our daily relationship with food happens through processes, ordinary gestures, and incorporated memories, identifying "experts," in the most complete sense of the word, becomes extremely problematic. This is why in this book I give so much importance to *naked* pleasure. It is therefore necessary to understand that the abilities to recognize and appreciate with respect to taste are qualified according to socially and culturally shared codes, but are not separable from interested assimilation, and, as such, must be articulated and understood within that context. So, even the most refined gastronomic critic is, at the end of the day, one of us, and vice versa, each one of us could become an expert, at least regarding certain foods. This description of different levels does not disqualify taste, but just the opposite: thanks to it, it has an enormous potential to draw the greatest amount of interest. Taste is a multimodal and flexible device, used in different ways in the most varied circumstances of everyday life. Tasting a beverage to verify its toxicity is not the same as tasting a premium wine: the tasting perception is always oriented according to the necessity established by the taster in that environment, the situation in which she finds herself. Dinner at a friend's house activates processes of attention and judgment with regard to food that are different than those that come into play in a famous three-star Michelin restaurant. Taste is both pleasure and knowledge; in some cases what's good is only related to pleasure, but in others, it is only related to knowledge; more often than not, it is related to both taken together. So "good" refers to a grammar of values where social and cultural codes claim as much space as instinct and personal experience do.

Third step: Beyond the subjective/objective paradigm, one needs to understand taste as an ecological system. It is this last observation that allows us to take a final step toward a new direction. Referring back to the historicity of the question of the subjectivity of taste, the subject/object paradigm was born in the modern age together with an anthropocentric epistemology according to which the human being is the measure of all things, the subject who knows, values, and judges objects. In the essay, I tried to conceive of taste according to a different paradigm by bringing back, in part, a wider vision, which can certainly be defined as systemically holistic or—as I prefer putting it—*ecological*. In other words, taste is a complex perceptive system, in the sense of a *multimodal ecological device*; one shouldn't conceive of it as a dualism between subject and object (the human being who tastes, on the one hand, and the object being tasted, on the other), but rather as an *ecological relationship*, an exchange of information among elements immersed in an environment. In this model, "good" goes beyond the question of subjective/objective since it always refers to a contextual experience, to the atmosphere in which the subject is located and included. "Good" is then the result of a triangulation between the perceiver, the perceived, and the environment—the context and the atmosphere—in which this relationship takes place. This allows us to conceive of differentiated situations and experiences. We can distinguish between at least four families of cases: (1) That in which "good" (in the sensorial sense) is also "good" (morally speaking). There are cases in which we truly desire the enjoyment of certain foods, and this desire corresponds to a legitimate state that makes us feel better from a moral standpoint. (2) That in which what is good for you corresponds to an appreciation of the ethics of food, which guides our sensorial and cultural education for pleasure. (3) That in which "good" corresponds to what is secure and known, to something that has a reference point for us. (4) That in which "good" corresponds to the exotic and the fascination of the unknown that does not offer familiar terms of comparison.

Each of these cases is legitimate within an aware and consistent perception. This consciousness I call *gustative wisdom*. The wisdom of taste is the flexible and elastic attitude that follows from acquiring the perceptive ability to differentiate the contaminations and the complex dynamics that are part of the tasting experience. It is a perceptive capacity that distinguishes the variables of the experience and that creates a feeling of awareness and satisfaction. Wisdom is the fruit of a long and complex journey toward increasing sensitivity, which in itself is not static. This is an ideal that should be understood more as a guide to explore experience, rather than as a perfect realization of it. Wisdom is the consciousness of the multiplicity of variables encountered during the experience of tasting food and so of the variables of "good," together with the ability to go through them, to move among them with openness and flexibility.

As I said, this book is the result of a long journey, not only an academic one, but also an existential one. Along this journey I have encountered many people whom I should thank for having helped me clarify the approach I have taken. The entire list would be very long, so I will limit myself to thanking those who either directly or indirectly, either personally or through their works, have given me important ideas, authentic examples, and vivid stimuli that I tried to assimilate and metabolize in my own way: Jacques Derrida, John Dewey, Aldo Gargani, Tim Ingold, Massimo Montanari, Carlo Petrini, Steven Shapin, Ludwig Wittgenstein. Finally, I am very grateful to Carolyn Korsmeyer for her precious help in the final editing of this English edition.

FOREWORD

MARGINALITY AND CENTRALITY

Nature and Culture. Subject and Object. Mind and Body. High and Low. These trite, contrasting, and time-honored pairs that still influence our way of thinking, and often crop up in our language, seem to dissolve like mist in the sun when we turn to Taste and wonder what it is, where it resides, and how this "sense," which has not always received the respect it deserves, actually works. There was, it must be noted, a current of Aristotelian thought—especially in its medieval revisitation—that raised Taste to a cognitive sense par excellence in virtue of its mixing with the object that, incorporated into the subject, can be discovered in its "true" and intimate essence. However, the vast majority of thinkers, not necessarily of Platonic ancestry, preferred to focus on the distal senses, sight above all, on the assumption that distance guarantees objectivity of judgment more than nearness does. To this, certain preconceived notions of a moral order were added, given the idea that the body, with its material instincts, is in itself dangerous, and that the senses that most forcefully engage it—the senses involved with touching—are the first to be mistrusted.

This distrust is not unwarranted because Taste, when thought about too much, can truly be revolutionary. It can undermine beliefs, certainties, and classifications—whatever human thought feeds on. The mechanism of perception can be described on the physiological level, which involves the individual with his or her sensations. It can be narrated historically, as Jean-Louis Flandrin did for the first time, reconstructing the "structures of Taste" in a collective key, that is, the trends, the choices that prevail in this or that society (open also to anthropological considerations). However, to hold together the complexity and many facets of this phenomenon, which is at the same time cultural and biological, individual and collective, ephemeral (because it exhausts itself in the act of eating) and stable (because it refers to socially shared values), it is necessary to rethink and revise quite a few parameters of our way of thinking. Nicola Perullo has been working on Taste for years and has finally decided to place it in the seemingly awkward dimension of *marginality*, laying claim, however, to a *centrality of marginality* that, besides constituting the specific character of Taste, seems to be a privileged (rather than embarrassing) and heuristically extremely interesting venue for rethinking the familiar concepts that we normally use. In this sense, thinking about Taste can indeed become intellectually revolutionary.

In this new book, Nicola Perullo outlines a theory of *experience* as a specific dimension of the aesthetics of Taste. Of Taste as an aesthetic *relationship* that indissolubly binds together the leading characters (the eater, what is eaten), but also the link between biology and culture, and the connection between gesture and thought.

I am a historian, hence hardly qualified to introduce an essay of such a strict philosophical nature as Nicola Perullo's. However, he has made it clear himself, albeit between the lines, that he intends to address a wider public and not just his direct colleagues (who can engage in a deeper reading and follow up on all the bibliographic references embedded in the exposition). The discussion thus proceeds with clear and accessible language, which is not just a rhetorical choice. It is also a project of philosophical thought—as I just said—founded on *experience*, which by definition belongs to everyone. Thinking about the not always obvious meanings of what we do, the often implicit notions that preside over our small daily choices, the depth of ideas that always accompany actions, is an exercise I find ethically as well as scientifically exemplary. It means recognizing the depth of each of our actions, even if it were a nonaction, or the *indifference* that constitutes a possible way of relating to food, which according to Perullo deserves no less attention than the pleasure principle, or the desire to know. This is why I like this book. This is why it reminds me of the way in which I, too, try to proceed when I write and speak about food (even though I start from different perspectives and use other methods): thinking and encouraging thought about the importance of things that seem small, but that contain the world, or at least reveal our relationship with the world (and with ourselves, since we are part of the world). Eating is easy, though not always. In any case, it is anything but trivial.

Massimo Montanari

TASTE AS EXPERIENCE

Children of a Lesser Sense?

Taste as an Aesthetic Relationship

> Do you think it *is* the part of a philosopher *to be concerned*
> *with such so-called pleasures as those of food and drink?*
> —SOCRATES, *Phaedo*, 64D

> *For me there is no radical distinction between the grand discourse*
> *on "the task" with all its dignity, and the reasons for wanting to go out*
> *to dinner with someone. They are not homogeneous questions,*
> *but I would not mark out a true opposition.*
> —JACQUES DERRIDA, *A Taste for the Secret*

THE PROJECT

This essay stems from a long exercise of observing the ways in which people encounter food and perceive it. This is a particular project that I need to clarify from the outset: the main topic of these pages will be *how* food is *absorbed* and assimilated according to an *aesthetic* approach. The meaning of "aesthetic" in this framework will become clear along the way, starting with this introduction. Allow me to anticipate a bit here by exclusion. My concern in this essay will not be food as an object in itself (for example, I will not inquire into the quality of food with regard to sensory profiles), but rather the *experience* of food—in a comprehensive and articulated sense. Condensed into a short and somewhat arcane formula, the essay's basic thesis could be put as follows: taste is situation, circumstance, and *ecological experience*. An ecological experience is what I call here an *aesthetic relationship*.

The title of the book refers to this formula even more synthetically: *Taste as Experience*, an explicit homage to John Dewey, who is one of the most important points of reference in this book and, in particular, his *Art as Experience*. I shall use *taste* here and not *tasting* as experience, as one would normally expect, for reasons I will explain along the way. So, what does it mean to say that taste is properly understood through experience, or rather that taste is an aesthetic relationship? Such a question cannot be answered with a pithy statement or a short definition. One needs patience and a spirit of observation. Understanding taste is a matter of learning to observe: to observe others but also oneself, because taste concerns everyone. Taste is not just *a* sense, nor is it only an emotion or an opinion. Above all, taste is not a thing. Taste needs to be *tried and tasted.*[1]

Taste, like theater, involves many actors and its procedural and dynamic nature comes together in scenes of particular meaning, as in a theatrical scene. I have my "primary scene" from which this idea has grown. A behavior I have always been attracted to and which still fascinates me is the facial expression of people ordering croissants and other pastries for breakfast at a coffee shop in the morning. There is hardly ever a neutral facial expression. Very often, the facial mimicry anticipates the satisfaction of a craving, by way of a vaguely complacent look cast on the object to be eaten, accompanied by the mere hint of a self-satisfied smile. Sometimes this mimicry is joined, in a single inseparable moment, by a shadow of guilt or dietary discomfort, which that interlocutory glance always reveals. This simple and everyday act caught my interest and I started comparing it with similar expressions such as that on the face of someone choosing from the menu at a restaurant, or of people ordering an inexpensive meal at a fast food restaurant after having stood in line for a long while. Over time, I put together an archive of images, made by differences in intent, in intensity, in tone, or in gesture. This now well-seasoned archive is the original source that sparked my thoughts on *taste*. It is the backbone of this book, grounded in the participation in and fascination for everyday and ordinary life.

In two previous works, I endeavored to reconstruct a genealogy that would establish a link between modern philosophical aesthetics and gastronomy, and organized a specific topic that could comprise this space theoretically (Perullo 2006, 2008). The present essay represents my own proposal, stemming from those two previous studies, within the viewpoint of relational aesthetics that characterizes taste. I will offer here a critical reflection on gustatory attitudes as aesthetic *encounters*—or at least as the most common and important ones—onto which my comprehensive theoretical proposal is grafted. It assigns an important and unexpected role to the experience of taste for food, but not in an exclusivist sense. This is not a book in praise of *gastromania*. It is not about praising the experience of taste as something exceptional and rare, or about understanding it as an instrument of power for individual claims of superiority or narcissistic exhibitions of skill. My proposal to value taste as an aesthetic relationship goes in a different direction. Drawing on the work of philosophers such as Epicurus and Montaigne, I intend to promote a more flexible and comprehensive approach, one that aims to be open, nimble, and nonspecialist, an approach that strives toward wisdom, as I explain in the last chapter. Believing in the value of food and taste does not mean subscribing to an exclusive lifestyle, nor does it imply becoming a food fetishist or a finicky "food extremist" obsessed with greed and gluttony. Rather, believing in the value of food and taste means having understood how it becomes possible to explore at least a large part of the sphere of everyday and ordinary human relations from a vital and fruitful perspective *through* the experience of food. This ambitious project aims to define a philosophy *not of* food, but rather *with* food, interpreted above all as aesthetics of taste: experiencing food and drink is ipso facto the comprehension of our ecological situation, how we face the environment, how the interconnections between us and the objects we eat, taste, and incorporate affect our being.

In the first place, I will try to answer two basic questions: How do we perceive food and drink? What are the presuppositions, the potentialities, and the limits of such perceptions? In addition to the primary scene mentioned above, I must add that many years of convivial, professional, and theoretical practice within the gastronomic scene have provided me with a plethora of different approaches to eating and drinking. Furthermore, many years of teaching wine tasting have allowed me to verify and also to directly experience the expectations and intentions that produce such approaches, as well as people's ensuing tics and aberrations. I found several of these aspects philosophically interesting and worthy of closer reflection. Two other factors also stimulated me, one professional and one personal.

First, we live at a moment in which Western society seems particularly interested in food, and we do so amid a series of complex and contaminated models, ideologies, and attitudes that go beyond the specific area and involve other aspects of culture and civilization. Conceptually tidying up this universe while at the same time offering a theoretical perspective on taste felt like a useful operation to me. In recent years, various insightful philosophical books on taste and the philosophy of food and wine have been written (Scruton 2010; Smith 2007; Korsmeyer 1999; Telfer 1996), and of course I am indebted to these authors. If my essay takes such references for granted, I have tried to explore a different way of looking at the philosophical appreciation of the experience of taste.

The second reason is personal, almost intimate. Jacques Derrida maintained that every system of thought—and, in general, every act of writing—stems from an autobiographical impulse. In this sense, he declared philosophy to be an *egodicea*, that is, an attempt to justify the course of one's life with rational arguments that transcend individual experience. Therefore, this essay is also the *egodicea* of a gastro-thinker, someone who for many years has needed to justify his passion for food and wine in a philosophical way. I experience gastronomy as a continuous and complete process of theoretical existence, inseparable from the search for meaning, thought, and effects. Food is my means, the refractive angle from which I interpret life, my search for humanity. All this is in line with Montaigne's dictum "we reach the same end by discrepant means."

I stated above that taste is not merely *a* sense; why? According to the mainstream of Western thought, taste is the simplest and the least interesting sense of our physiological apparatus, because it responds to a rather limited series of stimuli in comparison with the other senses. In truth, taste cannot be reduced to the chemesthetic sensations of the receptors in the oral cavity. Its process of sensorial elaboration in fact always involves the sense of smell and from time to time—depending on the specific type of function or purpose— all the other senses. This process is completed by the brain, on the basis of editing sensory data deriving from chemico-physical stimuli together with other pieces of information (cultural, educational, and contextual). Taste constitutes—to use a phrase coined by the psychologist James Gibson, who carried out pioneering studies in this field in the mid-twentieth century—a complex *perceptual system*. In other words, taste and smell are conventionally defined as chemical senses, because the *stimuli* to which the organs of the nose and mouth are first subjected derive from chemical compounds and are then processed by receptors. Yet taste and smell as *organs of perception* cannot be reduced to chemical senses. The process leading from a stimulus to its elaboration as sensation (that is, the immediate impression that corresponds to the quality and intensity of that stimulus), and from the sensation to its elaboration as *perception* (a higher-level modality organized into spatial and temporal information), is very complex and highly nuanced. Very simply put, like all the other senses, even taste does not occur within a physiological apparatus alone. Gustatory perception is a complex one, involving functions such as memory, recognition, and appreciation (Beauchamp 1997). Taste is therefore an intertwining of bodily and mental processes in constant interaction with the surrounding environment.

Acquiring such theoretical awareness gives great potential to a philosophy of food, but it is also a necessary step for a philosophy *with* food. If understanding taste as an aesthetic experience requires the knowledge of how the entire process works, if *scientifically* speaking taste is not a simple sense that can be reduced to a mere mechanical device consisting of a few basic flavors (scientists today count five: sweet, salty, sour, bitter, and umami, but new ones may join the list soon), *then* taste cannot be simple *philosophically* either. Rather, taste is a function of many individual, cultural, and social variables; but this fact produces valuable differences in every respect. And these differences require philosophical investigation, attention, and receptiveness in order to be clearly understood and experienced.

In the meantime, let us continue observing the customers at the coffee shop having breakfast. This scene is open to a wealth of interpretations regarding the meaning of experiencing food: the relationship between nutrition, pleasure, and enjoyment; the different life experiences of the actors being observed; the geographical and historical contingencies in which the scene takes place; as well as the quality and the final destination of the raw materials consumed. By playing detective in a coffee shop in the morning, one can collect much information about taste in terms of *value*, which cannot be simply reduced into quantitative and numeric factors. Because of this, I argue that a correct understanding of taste requires a *qualitative* dimension that calls for a specific *narrative* of every single experience, each with its own situated story and structure. The notions of value and quality are not exhaustive, but they form the backbone of the experiential and relational dimension of taste. So the present essay presents a combination of aesthetic reflections on the main theoretical problems regarding the narration of taste experiences. It goes without saying that this strategy is deliberately unsystematic: taste lies on the sidelines of systematic theorization, bound always to specifically biographical and autobiographical dimensions. Food is ingested and represents the only portion of the world we materially incorporate on a daily basis. It also constitutes one of our first, most relevant, and repeated relationships with the external world, and this is certainly enough to prevent us from treating it as a trivial object, or something to consider at a distance.

There are several positions regarding the theoretical status of taste. According to some scholars, taste can be objectified and systematized like any other object of study. According to others, however, its very characteristics prevent any possible systematization and produce a certain elusiveness, something that is considered as a limit to a serious treatment of taste. In my perspective, both positions are mistaken. On the one hand, taste represents a phenomenon unique to human experience, because the rapport we have with food is absolutely specific. It is for this reason that I believe that food philosophy is fully legitimate. On the other, one may explore that elusiveness or the marginality of taste with respect to our optical frame as a resource. The predominance of vision in the constitution of our grammar of thought is a serious issue. I do not think indeed that Western philosophy has typically neglected to take taste, cooking, and gastronomy into serious consideration merely because of a contingent ideological removal. The fact is that eating and drinking, like all daily activities, are at once very concrete and very fleeting activities; in fact, they appear more concrete and fleeting than many others, as they are necessary and subject to mechanisms of repetition, which tend to rob them of their meaningfulness. They are therefore sentenced to systematic marginality and theoretical transience. If we go back to the roots of the aesthetics of taste, however, it is true that gustatory taste has historically met with a twofold subordination. The first concerns the senses that are generally considered subordinate to the intellect. The second concerns the specific subordination of the so-called inferior senses (touch, taste, and smell) to the higher ones (sight and hearing). Both issues were questioned by the birth and growth of modern aesthetics in the eighteenth century, intended as "the science of sensible knowledge," according to Baumgarten's definition (from the Greek word *aísthesis*, "sensation," "perception"). The original project of aesthetics aimed to redefine and contrast them to a certain degree, by creating a space for a legitimate sensitivity, irreducible to an intellectual level. Historically, aesthetics and gastronomy share a common ground, a slightly rough terrain from where they began. But the neglect of taste can also be seen differently, as being linked to the very methods utilized in philosophy (at least in the Western tradition), as has been clearly shown by Korsmeyer (1999).

The domain of an aesthetics of taste, that is, a philosophical reflection geared toward understanding taste as an aesthetic experience, lies in this context: historical on the one hand, structural on the other. A historical vindication of taste is possible today only if understood with a profoundly philosophical acceptance of its marginality. The aesthetics of taste is therefore marginal because this sense cannot be understood exclusively through formulations and theories, yet its marginality should be embraced as a theoretical challenge. We live today in an age that could favor a similar train of thought. Of course, such conceptualization remains specific, exactly the kind specific to aesthetics as the science of singularities: taste as experience refers to specific cases, to empirical observations that become stories in a more hospitable and relaxed but no less real or compelling philosophical space. In other words, reflecting on taste also means reflecting *in* taste. If one lacks adequately lived experiences, it is difficult to come up with anything interesting to say on the subject.

Taste as *experience* must therefore be understood in two connected ways: experience as in having an experience in the world, as experiencing things of the world (as in becoming an expert), but also experience as living an experience, an inner experience, something that internally changes or enriches us. (In philosophy, these two meanings of experience are distinguished thanks to the German language, which has two distinct words, namely, *Erfahrung* and *Erlebnis*.) The French philosopher Gilles Deleuze, while explaining his interest in movies, once claimed that in order to find new ways for interrogating the world, philosophical thought ought to reflect not *on* but *in* the objects to be understood and dealt with. In other words, it should enter into a vivid and direct relationship with those objects, with that film seeming to offer that opportunity. This is even truer with taste, where there is a *tight* and very personal relationship between subject and object, a bond where the object is consumed *in* the body in order to sustain or transform the subject. Subject and object are not separate entities, but rather become a totally intertwined, dynamic, and complex in-between organism. The aesthetics of taste is therefore an aesthetics of relation and implication, an aesthetics that attempts to overcome the stiff and hypostatic resistances and dichotomies that exist between the entities of mind and body, subject and object, or nature and culture.

The multimodal and embedded character of taste—a blend of natural and cultural features—will be examined on various levels in the four chapters of the essay. For taste as an experience of pleasure, knowledge, and indifference espouses a dynamic conception of aesthetics, namely, the idea according to which there are gradual differences but not qualitative separations between the "lower" functions and simpler processes, such as those related to nutrition, and the "higher" and more complex ones, reflective thinking and the arts. Within the frame of this gradualist position, nature and culture are expressions of an environmental continuum with different and interacting players: humans, animals, plants, minerals, and everything elaborated and built by or with them. One of the main ideas underlying my proposal is that taste is always *ecologically* situated. Saying *ecologically* instead of *culturally* marks a difference: ecology refers to the environment, and according to Tim Ingold, whose position I totally agree with, an environment is a field of forces in which lively beings (as well as artifacts) grow (Ingold 2000, 2013). Human taste is therefore part of this *continuum*; it does not occupy a privileged position for being cultural with respect to the natural taste of other living beings. If anything, it is just a more elaborate structure. It makes no sense to oppose taste to nature and to claim that it is culture any more than the opposite makes sense. Taste is a relationship because it evolves: the childish pleasure we take in certain flavors or foods, which we retain or which suddenly floods back in adulthood, proves this all too well. As we will see especially in the first chapter, nature and culture are differential polarities, procedural articulations, and not static and objectified entities. Precisely for this reason, the approach to food and drink still practiced by some gastronomes, according to which the only way to appreciation lies in technical tasting skills possessed by a handful of experts, is questionable because it is—in an apparently paradoxical manner, as I'll attempt to show along the way—tied to a formalistic and abstract vision. A parallel can be drawn here with the conceptual shift in cooking, that is, that approach according to which the only thing that matters—for food and taste to be catalysts of values—is the ideas that transform food into what it becomes (Perullo 2013). This is neither a nostalgic suggestion nor an unlikely return to the so-called taste of origin as a natural pleasure; nor is it related to other charming but ideological simplifications. The point is rather to recognize and highlight the appropriateness of each *single* gustatory experience for the different ecological contexts in which it takes place and unfolds. There is no rule of thumb for how to taste, or for how to appreciate and enjoy.

There is not one way to taste correctly. In other words, in certain circumstances a kind of pleasure I will define as "naked" could be the most appropriate access to taste, regardless of specific cultural paradigms or ethical justifications. In other circumstances, however, this may not be the case.

Here the notion of context plays a decisive role. For example: lunch in a three-star restaurant is a very different experience from a quick bite at a roadside diner while on a trip, but it would be hasty to claim that only the first experience can offer gastronomic delight. In the first case, the pleasure offered and the attention required are of an intense and refined nature. But even everyday lunch *can* also be enjoyable. Not only are there sandwiches and sandwiches, some are very good indeed. There is also a more subtle reason related to the situation in which food is eaten. In fact, the sandwich itself might not be satisfactory, and one may feel culturally and sensorially far from fine dining, but this is not enough for rejecting such an experience or for denying its pleasure In fact, as one knows well there is also *negative* pleasure: in this instance, I can take pleasure even in recognizing that that sandwich is not good, yet I am hungry and I eat it. And satisfying my hunger is exactly what gives me pleasure here. Furthermore, I can derive enjoyment from being in a beautiful and hence satisfactory situation (for example, I am in the company of the person I am in love with) in such a way that the taste of the sandwich is completely charged with my amorous energy. Nonetheless, context does not play a hypostatic role here: it's not the deus ex machina of the whole story or, at least, not in a simple way. There are no rigid and absolute contexts indeed, as the notion of context is an open and variable one. Context is a set of connections established in a given scene, in a given theater of meaning; it is neither a foundation nor a fence, rather—to use a concept coined by Gibson—a net of *affordances*.

Addressing taste as an aesthetic experience also means understanding the dynamics of those affordances inserted into experience. I think a particular philosophical approach can offer a great help for this task. In this essay I have chosen to conduct my discussion in clear language and without the use of jargon, but the professional philosophers who read me will identify my approach as an eclectic combination of deconstruction, pragmatism, and anthropological approaches.

This book contains four chapters. They are stages in a process that is neither a straight nor an upward path, but rather a zigzagging one. The first three chapters—"Pleasure," "Knowledge," and "Indifference"—recount three different modes with which we can approach gustatory taste. Stemming from these three modes, the fourth chapter—"The Wisdom of Taste, the Taste of Wisdom"— is an elaboration of the experiential and existential attitude that captures the theoretical significance of the taste relationship with greater accuracy. This final attitude does not revoke any of the previous approaches but rather expands them into a wider framework. Each chapter explores the territory of *gusto* using different material, especially that derived from literature, philosophy, and personal experience. Only a few sources are explicitly gastronomical. There are two main reasons for this. First, I like to use every source I think may prove useful for analysis and reflection, without privileging any one genre. Second, I have sometimes found that my personal outlook is better represented by authors from other fields of learning rather than only gastronomy. Every chapter contains sections that investigate particular aspects of the approach taken into consideration.

The concepts of pleasure and knowledge are very complex ones and, obviously, are so broad and general in themselves that they cut across every field of human comprehension. In this essay, they almost become umbrella terms and are used exclusively as heuristic functions, to help map the whole possible spectrum of the experience of taste—at least as far as it can be put on paper, that is, modeled into a theory. In fact, pleasure and knowledge almost always intersect to a varying degree in concrete experience, modulating themselves along a spectrum from less to more, without absolute interruptions. A reflection on taste that starts from pleasure does, however, have one strong justification: our first contact with food is modulated by pleasure, a deep pleasure with its roots in the biocultural sphere of primary human drives, a sphere where pleasure and knowledge, need and desire, nutrition and taste are all one. One of our first aesthetic relationships with the external world is one where food is a source of both nourishment *and* enjoyment. There is a strong and precise connection between aesthetics and childhood (Dissanayake 2000) and food and taste can play an important role in evolutionary aesthetics. Even though a pure or naked pleasure is theoretically possible—at least from the perspective of the gustatory experience of the perceiver—it is very difficult to exclude more complex cognitive processes in the appreciation of certain foods and the rejection of others. Need, sensual pleasure, and knowledge often constitute a knot that is hard to untie. The Italian philosopher Giorgio Agamben defined taste as "pleasure that knows, knowledge that enjoys" (Agamben 2015). Accordingly, the separate treatment of these first two points of access—pleasure and knowledge—has a mainly descriptive and explanatory purpose, satisfying certain architectural constraints. This sketchiness will be extensively amplified through the use of examples and discussion.

If these first two modes of access to taste are, after all, obvious—it is always said that food is culture, and sometimes also that food is pleasure—the third is the dramatic turn of events in the aesthetics of taste as an aesthetic experience. Why should an essay promoting the aesthetic value of taste and defending the legitimacy of gustatory *expertise* also contain a thorough discussion and defense of indifference? All this may seem slightly bizarre. In support of the methodology of active observation underpinning my approach, experience has convinced me that it is also necessary to consider indifference in order to fully understand the experience of taste. Indifference to taste is not simply a lack of something (thoughtfulness, attention, or ability); it can also express feelings appropriate to the context and even necessary criticism. Furthermore, gustatory indifference is part of everyday life. Our perceptual apparatus, stimulated by food several times a day, does not always guarantee adequate levels of attention. Even indifference can thus serve as a resource for the overall experiential blueprint from which that procedural build-up called taste emerges. Indifference does not grow simply from static routine and is not always a trivial negation of values and ignorance. Together with pleasure and knowledge, it is part of a fluid experiential fabric, in which contaminations, entanglements, and multiple accesses are possible. Furthermore, indifference is necessary for achieving the concise and comprehensive attitude that is introduced in the last chapter of this essay with the concept of gustatory wisdom. Being a wise taster means having attained the realization of evolutionary change, of the finite and partial nature of experience, of the impossibility of severing ties with the deepest layers of our being that also emerge through taste and thus claim their rights. Gustatory wisdom is a flexible and elastic attitude that follows from the acquisition of the capacity to perceive differences, contaminations, and the complex dynamics inherent in taste experience. To put it in other words, here taste stands for a device that generates diplomatic skills and, at same time, that can improve our art of living.

Two more clarifications are in order. First, for reasons of competency, perspective, and space, I will not discuss any behavior directly associated with eating disorders such as anorexia, bulimia, and binge eating, nor I will discuss, except marginally, extreme behaviors such as fasting or cannibalism. I will instead focus on ordinary and everyday ways of gustatory perception: eating a donut, enjoying a piece of chocolate, drinking a glass of wine, exploring the local cuisine while traveling, or trying a traditional dish at a restaurant. Of course, I know that boundaries between normal and pathological may be slippery, and the description of certain experiences will touch upon areas that belong to the realm of pathology and are studied in psychology and medicine. But I have decided to leave any further exploration of these themes to the reader. The second point concerns a stylistic choice: although what follows is specifically and directly focused on taste and gastronomy, readers with a background in philosophy will be able to discern several theoretical references. Some are mentioned explicitly in the text, whereas others are not, so as not to weigh down the text. But I hope such references may also be of interest to readers who are not professionally engaged in the area of philosophy. I am convinced that taste is an open and wonderful topic in the practice of philosophy and, for this reason, I think that it can be taken as a quintessential case for contributing to contemporary thought and especially to aesthetics.

Food studies has developed in the Western academic world since the 1960s mainly thanks to anthropology (Claude Lévi-Strauss and Mary Douglas), history (Marc Bloch, Jean-Louis Flandrin, and Massimo Montanari), and sociology (Norbert Elias, Pierre Bourdieu, and Claude Fischler). Philosophy joined the group a little later through *gender studies* and *cultural studies* in the United States. The first groundbreaking and highly praiseworthy works (Curtin and Heldke 1992; Kass 1999) opened up possibilities for research in many areas. A few years later, books like those by Elizabeth Telfer (1996) and Carolyn Korsmeyer (1999) brought to light the full potential of food as a topic for philosophical inquiry. I believe that while the analytical approach of these works—especially Telfer's—point out very clearly the topic's theoretical issues, they nonetheless fail in two different aspects. First, because they still treat food as an object of analysis among others, regardless of its singularity, which makes it not only an object of study, but rather *a systematic set to be incorporated*. This methodology leaves out many things. Second, they do not develop a general perspective on what one may do with gustatory experiences in order to achieve alternative possibilities for a better quality of life. The transformative power of taste is therefore left out. These two issues are precisely those at stake in my essay. Before considering the heart of the matter, I ask you to bear with me a little longer while I sum up some very well-known difficulties and conflicts of a philosophical nature about taste. It is necessary to clear the path we wish to take of at least the major obstacles.

How is philosophical reflection on taste and gastronomy feasible? This is not a rhetorical question. Already Plato—in his dialogues *Phaedrus, Gorgias*, and *Phaedo*—refused to assign cookery the status of a science or an art. Plato compares cookery to rhetoric with respect to the false and seductive pleasures it provides. Cooking is an empirical activity aimed at seduction, since it only satisfies a basic need. It has nothing to do with knowledge because it does not proceed from general axioms, or with art because it does not satisfy any true and intellectual enjoyment. Its pleasures are physical, ephemeral, and unworthy of rational man: "*Do you think it is the part of a philosopher* to be concerned with such so-called pleasures as those of food and drink?" Socrates asks in the *Phaedo*. Here taste is at stake. In most of Western thought, the sense of taste—together with smell—is considered minor and inferior because it is more than proximal: its accomplishment is its intake. According to this view, which runs all the way through the history of Western culture, senses are divided into higher ones (sight and hearing) and lower ones (taste and smell). Touch usually stays in the middle, in an ambiguous position. In the Greek and the Christian tradition, sight—together with hearing, which is instead dominant in the Jewish tradition—is the noblest sense, because it is distal and, therefore, objective. Sight explores, knows, and measures entities in the distance. Controlling from a distance seems to be one of the main bases of objective knowledge: the *seen* entities become objects. Visual perception is the basis for much of our understanding of reality and for most of our relationships with things (Korsmeyer 1999), so much so that knowledge, as well as faith and beauty, is often depicted using visual metaphors: the word *idea* (mental *image*, etymologically derived from the Latin *video*, "to see"), the notion of *light* (which refers to beauty), and man as an *image of God*. Reading and listening are the true or at least the deepest accesses to knowledge, to faith, and to art. When aesthetics turned into philosophy of art, it mainly dealt in fact with visual and auditory arts, even less with touch (the decline of sculpture starting in the eighteenth century is telling), and not at all with taste and smell. As I already mentioned in this hierarchy, touch is in an ambiguous position, since it is evidently a sense of contact and proximity, but not of ingestion. According to some scholars, this difference is enough to grant touch a cognitive status, because it can explore the surface and the shape of things, without blending with them. In some modern philosophical systems—such as those of Descartes and Spinoza—touch is even a privileged sense. For Descartes, for example, all senses are attributable to touch on a physical basis (as the Greek philosopher Democritus maintained); taste is therefore a tactile sense. This position—a minority view in modern aesthetics— is very interesting in light of this book.

In a famous passage at the beginning of his *Aesthetics: Lectures on Fine Art*, Hegel states that "the sensuous aspect of art is related only to the two theoretical senses of sight and hearing, while smell, taste, and touch remain excluded from the enjoyment of art. For smell, taste, and touch have to do with matter as such and its immediately sensible qualities—smell with material volatility in air, taste with the material liquefaction of objects, touch with warmth, cold, smoothness, etc." (Hegel 1975, 38–39). Hegel is radical and also excludes touch from the realm of art; only sight and hearing produce aesthetic knowledge and pleasure. Taste and smell produce a pleasure that is physical, at least because it has developed by material processes that occurred into the body. Hegel and Plato completely agree on this point, and so does Kant, for whom a judgment of taste—an aesthetic judgment—is only given if the taste in question is a *metaphorical* one, that is, taste for beauty. Only artistic beauty and natural beauty allow for universal appreciation, tied to a pure, selfless, and necessary feeling, free from any material need and any urgent corporeal necessity. Much of modern aesthetics in the West took up these positions, perhaps varying them slightly, but often confirming the fundamental assumption of the exclusion or the subordination of taste and smell.

Of course, alternative positions occurred. Authors from the ancient world, the Middle Ages, and modern times have been willing to allow gustation into the realm of phenomena worthy of philosophical reflection, occasionally even using it for an alternative paradigm of knowledge. Epicurus—whom we will meet again in the next chapters—is the most famous representative and eponym of the positive and key role food plays in philosophy; but there are also libertines and materialists, and, interestingly, some medieval scholars attributed great importance to the palate. A monist and ecological conception of reality that goes beyond the dichotomy between the ideal and the real world can easily overcome the argument that places the distal senses as "superior" to the proximal ones. According to Gibson and Dewey, seeing and hearing, on the one hand, and touch, taste, and smell, on the other, are in fact different perceptual systems, with different functions, but they derive from the same psychophysical unit that developed during the course of evolution with respect to different skills. To put it differently, in a systemic approach, just as it is wrong to state that the brain is metaphysically superior to the hand, because a coevolutionary process between the development of the prehensile hand and the growth of the human brain occurred, it is also wrong to define sight as "superior" to taste and smell. Sight became more and more convenient and useful in the growing process of human beings. It is not so important to us now to recognize the scent of a blackberry bush as it is to recognize the noise of a car or the sight of a predator, such as a tiger. Or even the smell of gas in our apartment, informing us of the risk of an explosion.

Indeed, one can consider incorporation and assimilation a cognitively safer way of interacting with objects than sight, due to the assumption that epistemic certainty may require exploration by contact (a food may seem cold to the eye, only contact will tell me if it is hot). Even the inventor of the term *aesthetics*, the Leibnizian Baumgarten, left a possibility for the palate: aesthetics as "the science of sensible knowledge" referred to all senses. In the original project, aesthetics was to be the science of all arts, including the beautiful ones, as well as the practical and useful ones. However, as I already mentioned, after its birth Western aesthetics turned primarily to elaborating the *intangible* aspects of art. Thus, Epicurean thought, as well as that of thinkers such as Montaigne, remained marginal and secondary. And even if the cognitive ennobling of gustatory taste were thought to be possible, it does not imply its free and unlimited cultivation and circulation: the paradigm of moderation—*la giusta misura*—became a precept of the highest importance also for those who claimed the legitimacy of food pleasures. David Hume, who carefully took taste and the palate into account for his explanation of aesthetic appreciation, wrote that a "very delicate palate, on many occasions, may be a great inconvenience both to a man himself and to his friends: But a delicate taste of wit or beauty must always be a desirable quality; because it is the source of all the finest and most innocent enjoyments, of which human nature is susceptible" (Hume 1909–14, §17). The moral of the story is that an expert in visual arts will never be accused of knowing too much, yet it is easy to see how the intake of food beyond a certain measure is considered, outside of health issues, to be *ethically* and *politically* dangerous.

Are the views of Platonic philosophy, of Kantian and Hegelian aesthetics on the value of gustatory taste mere relics of the past? Unfortunately not. Two recent examples from Italian journalism will suffice to demonstrate this. The first appeared in the newspaper *La Stampa* on September 26, 2007, in an op-ed by the Spanish philosopher Fernando Savater titled "L'arte della digestione" (The art of digestion). In this article, Savater criticized the way in which today the media celebrates gastronomy and chefs, taking the cue from a number of meetings on creative cooking and polemicizing in particular using the idea of cooking as an art form, promoted in the last decade by the great chef Ferran Adrià. At the heart of his argument, Savater claimed that food "is an honest craft, not an artistic creation whose goal is not to satisfy the mere senses, but to awaken feelings and encourage the discovery of new meaning. The highest effect of a dish is to pleasantly satiate hunger; true art, in reality, begins later." Savater fused here the Platonic argument with the Hegelian and Kantian one: art has nothing to do with material sensitivity except as an interim stage. Seeing and hearing actually serve as a go-between for the spiritual and ethereal feeling of beauty. The strategy I propose in this essay is quite the opposite paradigm: I do not deny the importance of the satisfaction of hunger, but rather suggest that satiating hunger *can be* a way to awaken feelings, create emotions, and enrich one's own life with new meanings (Perullo 2013). The second example was published in the Sunday insert of *Il Sole 24 Ore* on March 15, 2009. With a polemic sideswipe at unnecessary spending in times of crisis, the author also picks on Ferran Adrià, the true bogeyman of any critic of the artistic value of gastronomy, "who serves the most sophisticated and most expensive food in the world in his restaurant." (By the way, this second bit of information is objectively false, it was never true that Adrià's restaurant—which definitively closed its doors on July 30, 2011—was the most expensive one in the world.) The article quoted the Catalan chef's answer to the question regarding the *ethical* legitimacy of spending about two or three hundred Euros for a dinner. According to Adrià, the decision of who goes to a certain kind of restaurant was to be framed in a different complex of issues. Eating at Adrià is not about going out for dinner, but rather about wanting to indulge in an overall experience that is not only sensory but also cultural, aesthetic, and—in this case—even artistic. From this perspective, the choice is as legitimate as spending one's money to attend a premiere at La Scala or a major sporting event, or even to buy a pair of designer slacks. This (not only legitimate but also philosophically sound) consideration was greeted by the columnist with "Adrià, give us a break! There is no gallery in your restaurant, if a client does not appreciate your liquid nitrogen mozzarella she cannot even whistle, and in any case you will have to concede that a designer dress lasts a little longer than a dinner." In a presumptuous and mocking tone, three arguments are used here to confute the deep cultural value of gustatory taste. The first one is that gastronomy is not comparable to art, because "true" art is something altogether different. It is supposedly concerned with spiritual, universal, and disinterested pleasures, not with bodily, singular, and interested ones. The second one is that gastronomy is not comparable to true leisure and genuinely entertaining practices either, such as going to the stadium, where the audience can vent its feelings by whistling. Here gustatory taste and fine dining are curiously enough presented as practices that are empty and boring at the same time, *hardly serious* if compared to knowledge and art but paradoxically also *too serious* with respect to leisure and fun. The third argument—one of the most classic objections against the value of gastronomy—is that gustatory pleasures are not comparable to clothing and couture either, because unquestionably clothes last longer than a meal; they are less perishable items and, therefore, a better investment. The *Consumption Exclusion Thesis* (Monroe 2007) still looms large in the ordinary perception of the (in)comparable values of food and art. Even today, in the age of performance arts, there is a widespread conception according to which a work of art—as an object or as an experience—is a valuable fact because it is lasting, in terms of its permanence, of its cultural memory, and of its *storage*. The prejudice that a dish and a meal are quickly consumed is still ongoing, although everything today clearly indicates that this is not the case (digital memory, mediatization, narration on one side; dietetics and political issues about food hold everyone's attention) (Perullo 2013).

The objections against gustatory taste thus fall into three categories: epistemological (taste belongs to the minor senses, cooking belongs to the empirical activities); aesthetic (true art *versus* crafts or applied arts); ethical (the dangers of physical pleasure, compliance to animal instincts, gluttony and greed). Today, these objections seem threadbare, both from a theoretical and from a practical point of view. The idea of any rigid definition of art was called into question from the beginning of the twentieth century onward by many authors (including, Benjamin, Wittgenstein, Dewey, and Danto, to name but a few from different philosophical areas) and now into the domain of aesthetics it is almost commonsense. In the twentieth century, the modern separation between the fine arts and crafts, between theoretical and practical activities, was also called into question. More recently, some scholars like the sociologist Richard Sennett and the anthropologist Tim Ingold have proposed a conception of art in its original and most long-lived meaning, that of skillful making and technique (*téchne*). Art, in the ancient world and throughout the Middle Ages at least up until the Renaissance, was mainly know-how, and was produced according to rules. It therefore expressed the technical capacity and dexterity to make objects with superior care and recognized ability, but within an established code that served as a paradigm. This is an interesting consideration for our specific topic: cooking is certainly a good example of knowing how to do something according to rules, hence a pertinent example of art as skillful making. Therefore, its exclusion from the *artworld* would seem wrong. Moreover, the representation of the gastronome as someone boring and overweight, if, on one hand, occasionally true, is, on the other, often a caricature produced by someone who holds the whole subject in disregard. Not all gastronomes are dull and ignorant, just as not all philosophers and journalists are intelligent and brilliant. Let us once again take Ferran Adrià as an example, the most discussed and probably least directly "tasted" chef in the history of cooking. Many of his critics, as we have seen, have never set foot in his restaurant (and not even in restaurants comparable to his), nor do they know anything precise about his techniques or about the history of cuisine. Adrià has become the symbol of artistic cuisine, and furthermore has become so in the modern sense of art, which means creativity, originality, and imagination. He was, in 2007, the first chef to be invited as an artist to the *Documenta* exhibition (Hamilton and Todolì 2009). Although the contemporary *artworld* accepted this, it was feared and opposed by many others. Why? In this essay, I will suggest that the reasons are psychological and historical rather than theoretical. Finally, even the argument that gustatory taste is an ephemeral and fleeting pleasure has been strongly questioned. Taking, as it were, the bull by the horns, how could one measure the length and also the intensity of pleasure? Proust's *madeleine* is the easiest example of a different possibility, applying the same paradigm in which taste can evoke and express feelings, sentiments, and memories. It can be a resurfacing of emotional states presumed to have been overcome and forgotten. Food's potential depth of pleasure and taste can also be substantiated through memory and, in any case, a short but intense experience does not necessarily produce less significant pleasure.

Much of twentieth-century aesthetics has contemplated these questions and tried to provide answers to deconstruct both the Kantian arguments on the judgment of taste and the Hegelian ones on aesthetics as philosophy of art based on the paradigm of visual and auditory perception. These responses provide us with the technical tools that can be applied to a philosophical program in which food is based on taste as a relational experience. If we put these tools to use, it becomes possible to overcome contemplative aesthetics, which exclude the body and gustatory pleasures from the realm of philosophy. If, therefore, a complex project and good arguments are necessary in theoretical terms, on the practical side things are much easier and speak for themselves.

POSSIBILITIES AND PERSPECTIVES

Attributing an aesthetic value to gustatory perception is an option that falls under a more general theoretical perspective. Food constitutes an exceptional field of investigation for a coevolutionary and ecological concept of culture. Taste as an aesthetic experience also represents a possibility of promoting a systemic relationship between food fruition (consumption) and food production. Mass industrial production has progressively deprived the human body of the possibility of autonomously producing and processing food by replacing it with machines. This modern change has been obviously beneficial for many aspects of human life, and has allowed more and better food to reach more people. Under the lens of taste experience, however, that shift of paradigm has often led to a perceptive impoverishment, resulting in an increasing distance between production and consumption. In modern agriculture, this is defined as a "long production chain," with no direct relationship between the eater and the eaten, no information, no knowledge of the sources and of the processes of food making. It has become very difficult to think of food in relational terms, and it is also for this reason that we frequently witness total indifference to taste, with the production of anonymous food, of which nothing is known and which is prone to a purely instrumental approach. In the last two centuries the value attributed to practical skills, especially as far as production is concerned, has steadily decreased. It has become subordinate to design-related intellectual skills and mechanical production (Ingold 2000; Sennett 2009). From this point of view, the *Encyclopédie ou Dictionnaire raisonné des sciences, des arts et des métiers*, published between 1751 and 1772 under the direction of Diderot and D'Alembert, is one of the last attempts to uphold the importance of these skills and of the technical expertise, acquired with patience and experience, that they require. The subordination of practical skills to intellectual abilities in production runs parallel to the subordination of taste to sight: the "minor" senses refer to practical and marginal skills compared to the constituting processes of the master narrative of modernity, which instead stipulates the "major" senses as the natural instruments for scientific and technological progress.

However, industrial food production is neither good nor bad in itself: its meaning and its value lie in the development of human thinking under a technological guise that, as such, is a great adaptive and evolutionary resource. Nevertheless, technological development does not entail the dismissal of the capacity and skills of the human body in terms of its expression of wants and primary desires, primarily in food making and eating. In the present age, technology can also allow for a fulfilling and intense quality in the aesthetic relationship between human beings and food. It all depends on how technology is used, and on the experiential and social context in which it operates. Gustatory relational aesthetics can play a crucial role for improving awareness of the systemic connection between production and consumption.

The word *taste* has undergone a semantic shift since the middle of the seventeenth century, passing from identifying a *natural* sense assigned to the recognition and appreciation of edible substances to expressing a *cultural sensitivity* entrusted with the evaluation of natural beauty and, above all, works of art. This shift from the literal to the metaphorical strongly affected the subordination of the taste with respect to the other senses. By the eighteenth century, gastronomy had carved out a minor niche for itself in the context of shared practices, hobbies, and recreational activities. Since then, gastronomes have been mostly affluent professionals, dandies, refined connoisseurs, collectors, and journalists. The intellectual-gastronome is as rare as he or she is evanescent. In this light, things are beginning to change: gastronomy and cuisine are gaining ground and many important chefs are becoming highly visible public figures comparable to pop stars and contemporary artists. This contamination between pop culture, material practices, and the Academy—judged, as usual, with moral contempt by purists of thought—offers new potential for gastronomy. In this essay, I will propose a promotion of taste through a *lowering strategy*: on the one hand by accepting its marginal status, and on the other hand by developing an alternative and critical concept of making and eating food. Gastronomy here is seen not as a social club for acquiescent gentlemen, but rather as a dynamic space in which philosophy, humanities, arts, and natural sciences can reflect on their own times.

Strategies for valuing taste cannot be planned by overthrowing the hierarchy of the perceptible and upsetting the axiological order between minor senses and major senses. The fact that taste is marginal to thought, to knowledge, and to art is not due to vast carelessness, negligence, or a major conspiracy (as the French philosopher Michel Onfray, author of many books advocating the liberation of physical pleasure and taste, is inclined to think). It is not necessary to line up the good guys (the Epicureans, the materialists, the libertines, Feuerbach, Nietzsche, and so on) and the bad guys (the Platonists, the idealists, the ascetics). Nor is it necessary for gastronomy to gain admission to the realm of institutional modern art. Instead, taste and cooking should be used to contribute to a redefinition of the boundaries of art (Perullo 2013). Just as the German philosopher Walter Benjamin advised in his essay "The Work of Art in the Age of Mechanical Reproduction" from 1936, in order to be able to consider cinema as an art form, it is not necessary to turn it into something it is not (for example, a refined form of painting or theater); instead, it is necessary to expand the domain of art, to rethink it on a new basis (Benjamin 2008). The same will happen to gastronomy if a reassessment of taste comes about by way of a *lowering strategy*, consisting in knocking art off its pedestal and, at the same time, in taking taste experiences as aesthetic ones (Saito 2007). This leads to a consequential shift from a subject/object paradigm of knowledge to an ecological one, a "knowing from the inside" perspective as Tim Ingold (2013) calls it.

Today a popular and counterproductive misunderstanding exists. Asserting a distinction between cuisine as art and cooking as "simple" craftsmanship means implying a highly problematic (and outdated) distinction between the creations of the mind and the repetitive and mechanical executions of the hand and body. In this frame, a hierarchical distinction would seem to exist between material techniques and skills—chopping, touching, cooking, and tasting—and conceptual design and ideas. According to this view, the chef is a designer or even a conceptual artist. Thus, "normal" and ordinary cooking would not fall under the category of artistic cuisine, which would only be considered as the expression of exceptional moments originated by the creative mind of a chef. This setting is deeply flawed and confusing and, in the end, it leaves everything just as it was. There are valid theoretical and ethical reasons to refute it. In fact, on the one hand identifying the creative process only as an intuitive act of a mind is wrong: creating artifacts is a complex process made mostly of real, physical work *with* the original idea. On the other hand, the hierarchy of fine dining (cuisine) and ordinary cooking implies social and political issues. As in the *artworld*, the *gastroworld* is subject to codes drawn up by a few people, a few critics, and a few cooks.

It is therefore necessary to proceed differently and change the perspective. There are two steps to the strategy of the aesthetics of taste as experience. The first is the unrelenting emphasis on the value of marginality, in all its possible forms. This is the key to reconsidering established boundaries and customary codes. Changing the signs on the marginality of taste perception means accepting its paradoxically parasitic nature: taste is the paradigm of *embodied knowledge*, which originates and develops in *and* through the body, and which is not conceivable otherwise. But taste also needs observation, reflection, and introspection, on the one hand, and expression, sharing, and concepts in order to be communicated, on the other hand. The second, even more exciting step involves embracing a different concept of aesthetic value. This concept takes the functional, instrumental, ordinary characteristics of food to the most extreme consequences: the acts of being ingested, assimilated, and metabolized should become the cornerstone of the new aesthetic values of food. In other words, the gustatory process of ingesting, assimilating, and metabolizing plays a key role for the aesthetic value of taste. Instead of classic aesthetic values such as formal beauty, elegance, and harmony forged on distal contemplation (because these objects are never ingested), here we come face to face with the specific domain of eating and tasting. Eating *well* is an aesthetic value, but "well" does not mean accommodating a value to a standard of reference borrowed from another field. Rather, "well" has to do with the contact of food with our internal tissues, with the juices that make it digestible, with the channels that transport it to where it can be processed. This move will allow enhancing the taste experience *as such*, not as more or less comparable to the intellectual (and conventionally aesthetic) ones.

Pleasure, knowledge, and indifference are the three main entryways to taste experiences, from the highest intensity and attention to its total absence. I propose to accompany the reader on a journey into this territory. Pleasure goes back first of all to the primary, infantile, instinctual, *naked* stage of our relationship with food, a stage that is never completely and definitively overcome: pleasure is never neglected. Food is not only—and this statement is equivalent to: cannot be simply reduced to—a cultural construct. In other words, eating is an activity in which, in many respects and from time to time, something like "nature" emerges. After pleasure, knowledge leads us to our conscious intentions, to adulthood, and to the evolution of culture: taste gets *dressed*. This is a vast and fascinating field, thanks to which the problems of language, identity, authenticity, different preferences, and appreciation can be addressed. Finally, indifference refers to the negation, suspension, or suppression of taste for many different reasons. In this experience, gustatory attention leaves the scene and food is left to perform its purely nutritional and energy-providing function. This is a necessary integration of the experience of eating, without which one would understand nothing of taste as an aesthetic perception. Understanding these three modes of access encourages what I suggest calling the *wisdom of taste*, a perceptual ability that assimilates the variables of eating experience and reconciles them with a mindful awareness. Wisdom is the outcome of endless self-enhancement and is a dynamic, not static, condition. It can be depicted better as a guide for the continuous exploration of experience than as a perfectly attained state.

Understanding the taste experience as a whole does not mean isolating it from its ordinary dimension. Taste does not have to be ennobled and does not have to become something other than itself. Rather, it is integrated into a philosophy *with* food, which is close to an aesthetics of everyday life (Saito 2007). Taste as aesthetic relationship lies on the margins of theory. It can also be understood as a theory of the margins. It is an elusive and ethereal object of reflection, precisely because of its evidence, its universality, and its ordinariness. After all, Ludwig Wittgenstein said that the most important aspects of things are hidden because of their simplicity and familiarity. And Roland Barthes stated in turn that we do not see our own food or, worse, we assume that it is insignificant and trivial. So let's start observing and perceiving our daily food with open-mindedness, patience, and confidence.

First Mode of Access

Pleasure

The beginning and root of every good is the pleasure of the stomach.
Even wisdom and the refinements are referable to this.
—EPICURUS (ATHEN.)

The daily intake of food is an everyday and ordinary activity that can be seen under different perspectives. One perspective is biological: the process of eating is regulated by biological mechanisms of the brain. Eating and drinking are actions that activate brain functions related to emotions and pleasure (Beauchamp and Bartoshuk 1997; Halpern 2005; Holley 2006). Another perspective, related to the first one, is psychological: a human being's—or maybe any living being's—first *emotional* input is food. Through the assumption and consumption of food, the infant develops a fundamental relationship with its mother in the prenatal and the postnatal phase (Mennella, Jagnow, and Beauchamp 2001). This fact, which has always been common knowledge and is confirmed both by behavioral psychology and by cognitive science, would seem sufficient to justify pleasure as the initial argument of an essay on the aesthetics of food. Actually, this is the first problematic aspect. In the humanities, medicine, and *nutritional science*, taste is treated from different angles, but curiously enough, pleasure is most often not part of the picture. In this chapter, I will follow the indications of common knowledge and of psychology in designing an aesthetics of gustatory perception. The first question to ask is: Can the experience of food convey only pleasure? Can we feel pleasure for something about which we know nothing precise? Certainly, and that is the most common experience with food. Let us imagine the desire for a cold beer in the middle of summer. The treat is *a cold* beer and not *that beer* in particular: because it is a *beer*, a generic one, and because of the thermal perception it exudes. Or the desire for chocolate: a pure craving for sugar, cocoa, and theobromine. And why not acknowledge that, at times, we like wine for its inebriating effects, and not only for its qualitative and sensory characteristics? These are, in fact, ordinary experiences that every child has had (not with beer and wine, of course) even when we know nothing about the source of food and its cultural physiognomy. This also happens when we go abroad and we are offered unusual or exotic food.

The access to food *via* pleasure would thus seem a solidly plotted course, an easy path, but that is not the case. Over the course of time, religious, cultural, and philosophical traditions have devoted themselves to establishing the subordination of pleasure to ethics and knowledge, in particular with respect to the danger it represents (Shapin 1998). And this is one of the reasons for the social subordination of food and taste; in fact, it seems very difficult to strip food of its hedonic dimension. Nonetheless, a way out of this impasse seems to have opened up in recent decades by considering the taste of food as *cultural*. This approach has produced the praiseworthy result of attracting great attention to food, by the academic establishment, institutions, politics, and the media, yet it paradoxically comes with a high risk: the denial of pleasure. Today, many food scholars have no interest whatsoever in the pleasure of food. Entire conferences dedicated to the topics of food culture, taste, and cuisine conclude with pathetic, bland, and thoughtless dinner receptions, as if to suggest that yes, it is important *to talk* about it, but do not expect to practice and experience it with satisfaction and pleasure. Viewing food as culture can in fact be positive evidence or a major misunderstanding that stems from an erroneous contraposition of nature and culture. The joy of food must recover its inaugural role,

both in biological and in cultural terms. We have to start by understanding the aesthetic relationship through this first mode of access.
We eat before we speak. Food is prior to language. A human being's
first aesthetic input, before language, before the assimilation of cultural codes, is the enjoyment of food. Were it for this alone, taste as
pleasure would be a fundamental way of feeling and of perceiving.
There is something more: pleasure does not disappear with evolution, neither on an individual level nor from the species as a whole.
Sometimes pleasure returns and expresses ways of accessing taste,
which we must then deal with.

If all perception—including gustatory perception—is always situated, influenced, and mediated, if, to put it in other words, perception
is always ecological, this does not imply that *specific* and differentiated
perceptive experiences are not possible. What I want to explore here
is how there are differences from the "inside" perspective of the perceiver, and how an experience is lived and fulfilled. There is a pleasure that we could define as *naked*, childlike, that is not lived as socially
constituted, and that refers to very deep levels of our psychophysical
being, levels we struggle to rationally dominate and manage according
to adult codes that in many other cases govern our actions.

Pleasure, Enjoyment, and Intelligence

In 1970, a team of psychologists at Stanford University began one
of the longest-running experiments in behavioral psychology: the
"marshmallow experiment," conducted on about six hundred children, then aged four. The purpose of the experiment was to study
the processes of delayed gratification. The children were led into
a room, offered a marshmallow, and told, "If you don't eat the
marshmallow now, in fifteen minutes I'll bring you another one."
Researchers wanted to verify the correlation between the capacity to resist temptation—thus delaying gratification—and an individual's behavior in the following years. The same participants were
then periodically subjected to more trials, and the results seemed
to indicate that the greater the ability to resist sweets, the greater

the ability to succeed first in school and then at work and in social relationships (Casey et al. 2011). The explicit and implicit meanings of this experiment are numerous. They do not, in fact, concern the cognitive and emotional implications of food alone, but also the social and political ones: What does it mean to "be successful"? What are the benchmarks for the test's "positive" evaluation? Although these questions go beyond the direct purpose of the experiment, they are not without importance for our inquiry on taste as an aesthetic relationship. This test, in fact, seems to substantiate the view that moderation and control of taste are the only possibilities for a socially and individually virtuous life.

A notable philosophical tradition considers sensual pleasure—namely, sex pleasures and food pleasures—as an obstacle to knowledge and to intelligence. In a coevolutionary paradigm, however, mind and body are not two separate entities but representations of the same biopsychic unit. Along the same line, pleasure and intelligence are modulations of the ecological and adaptive process that characterizes human life. We must insist on this connection to avoid the mistake of believing that the only chance for pleasure to turn into a shared value is its rarefaction and dematerialization into pure internal aesthetic pleasures. (Dematerializing pleasure was exactly Kant's brilliant move in the *Critique of Judgment*.) The Belgian writer Amélie Nothomb agrees with us regarding the misconception of the disembodiment of pleasure and the union between sensuality and intelligence: "There has always been a large group of imbeciles opposing sensuality to intelligence. They inhabit a vicious circle: they deny themselves any extravagance to exalt their intellect, and the result is they diminish their intellect" (Nothomb 2003, 27). The pleasure of food is an ideal access for promoting the virtuous cycle of sensual enjoyment and intelligence, because food is a daily, necessary, and universal pleasure, but with a vast number of variables that summon human imagination. Put in this frame, the question of moderation is not an alibi for neglect; rather, it assumes a different connotation for the cultivation of one's life.

Pleasure, enjoyment, and desire—carefully kept separate in the tradition of contemplative aesthetics—permeate one another seamlessly in food, or rather they are different facets of the same thing. In Noth-omb's works, the notion of pleasure crops up everywhere. In her writing, pleasure—very often just gustatory pleasure—plays a funda-mental role. In one of her most important autobiographical novels, *The Character of Rain*, Nothomb narrates her own primal scene. In the first pages, she describes her true initiation into life at the age of two and a half. Before then, she remembers having been plant material ("Your child is a vegetable," the doctors judge [Nothomb 2003, 4]) or even less: plants at least possess a primitive sensibility that leads them to react to external stimuli, but the little girl is "wholly and completely impassive" (5), a being "without sight" walled into abso-lute ontological autism. Heretically, the narrator compares this con-dition to that of God: Amélie feels like God because God is a tube, inertia without movement, and pure passivity. This hydraulic cavity is home to a neutral and purely energetic absorption of food: no taste or smell is attached to the act of ingestion. In this narrative process, God is on the opposite side of taste. The real "birth" of Amélie therefore only takes place at the age of two and a half, thanks to an experience of pure pleasure, a delight: "Sweetness rose to God's head and tore at its brain, forcing out a voice it had never before heard: It is I! I'm talking! I'm not an 'it,' I'm a 'me'! You can no longer say 'it' when you talk about yourself. You have to say 'me.' And I am your best friend. I'm the one who gives you pleasure" (24). Pleasure transforms mere passivity into active sensibility, into perception: the awareness and voluptuous abandonment to the pure *material substance* of a food lead to an upheaval that promotes the psychophysical processes of active life, identity, and language. This pleasure is obviously not intellectual, but rather pure sensitive enjoyment. Yet which food gives such plea-sure as to rouse the child from her lethargy? A bar of white choco-late skillfully administered without the parents' knowledge by her paternal grandmother. By shared opinion, in our society chocolate is the food of pleasure par excellence: a "category of the world" (to use Barthes's [1997, 23] expression), a universal stimulant. This white bar full of sugar, "good, sweet, and velvety," leads Amélie from inertia to memory and language, to an intelligence that phenomenalizes in sight: "life begins with sight" (2).

The novel's narrative proposes a hierarchical turnaround of the perceptible: if matter changes, passive inertia, the neutral, the tasteless, and the monotonous (the food is "always the same") are on God's side. This means that the logos, the spoken word, is not the origin of life. In other words, it is not spiritual substance that animates human beings, making them as such and differentiating them from vegetative life, as held by the Judeo-Christian and the Greco-Roman tradition. On the contrary, Nothomb postulates that material pleasure experienced through food is essential to the human experience. Therefore, in the beginning, there was emotion as sensory pleasure rather than logos. But this would mean that the human experience originates with the senses of touch and taste, and not the distal ones. Human experience starts with a *relationship*, since pleasure is born from the contact between two beings, and this relationship is *aesthetic*, since hedonic input is involved. Thus, the aesthetic relationship *as* pleasure triggers the plastic responsiveness of perception and opens up to memory, intelligence, awareness, and language, the functions that manifest themselves in sight. This primary relationship that becomes manifest in abandonment to voluptuous pleasure— narrated in such an exemplary fashion by the Belgian writer—stems from the depths of our biological human nature and, as such, is something that everyone should have experienced, especially individuals who have a positive and passionate relationship with food: an engrossing and surprising pleasure, a captivating burst of flavor (which can also activate memories, as we will see). Nevertheless, the path of "naked" pleasure is not without context. Even naked pleasure is an ecological perception. Enhancing the perceptual experience of gustatory naked pleasures does not, therefore, mean adhering to a naive form of naturalism. The pleasure of food is a vehicle for a more expansive urge, which points to a human being's first vital and adaptive functions: hunger for food is related to a more general hunger, an evolutionary energy (in philosophical terms, the *conatus*) that drifts toward the gratification of needs and desires. Regarding the theoretical importance of the nutritive function, the French philosopher Emmanuel Lévinas wrote: "Of course we don't live in order to eat, but it is not really true to say that we eat in order to live" (1988, 20).

This thought reminds us that food is not a fuel or an inert medium, and proposes a philosophy of hunger, or better a philosophy *through* hunger. *Being hungry* means desiring at a deep level, where the physical and the metaphysical coincide. Nothomb, from her point of view and with different words, writes: "Superhunger . . . wants the best, the most delectable, the most splendid, and it sets out to find out in every area of pleasure" (2006, 15). And further: "'Too sweet': the expression seems as absurd to me as 'too beautiful' or 'too much in love.' There are no things that are too beautiful: there are only perceptions whose hunger for beauty is half-hearted" (16).

In *The Character of Rain*, the original emotion that kindles intelligence is the result of a precise and intentional plan by a third party, the paternal grandmother. The grandmother plays the role of martyr and revealer of secrets. In fact, once she has handed her granddaughter the key for sight and consciousness, she immediately dies, because the act of passing on the secrets of pleasure also saves the child from death: "I sat on the stairs, thinking about my grandmother and her white chocolate. She had helped liberate me from death, and soon after it was her turn" (Nothomb 2003, 42). The gustative relationship drawn from the encounter with a bar of white chocolate takes place in a situation where a primary hedonic drive appears together with contextual elements. Therefore, the experience of naked pleasure is ecologically lived and fulfilled and emerges from a whole narrative process. The perceiver's perspective is peculiar here, and this peculiarity is what the aesthetics of taste as experience plans to analyze and enhance. Taste as experience loves differences more than analogies. In another autobiographical novel, *The Life of Hunger*, the Belgian writer comes back to chocolate, further specifying its value and changing its meaning with respect to the encounter between pleasure and divinity. Here, God no longer possesses the passive inertia of a water pipe, that is, purely neutral and tasteless matter, but God actually becomes a *gustative relationship*, an encounter between the perceiver and the matter perceived. "Is it not enough to have some very good chocolate in your mouth, not only to believe in God, but also to feel that one is in his presence? God isn't chocolate, he's the encounter between chocolate and a palate capable of appreciating it. God was me in a state of pleasure or potential pleasure: therefore he was me all the time" (Nothomb 2006, 21). The sin of gluttony is nullified, the relationship sanctifies delight. The experience of pleasure is a union between the self and the divine. However—Nothomb specifies—reaching such heights requires great capacities "and a palate capable of appreciating" the power of chocolate. Unlike what we saw in *The Character of Rain*, pleasure here explicitly goes hand in hand with a code of appreciation, an expertise. This is a subtle but significant difference, which points in the direction of the main thesis of this essay: every taste experience is embedded in a theater of meaning, an ecological situation from which it grows and develops, making it specific and different from other experiences. In the example just mentioned, clearly pleasure and knowledge are intertwined. Perhaps more than any other substance, chocolate lends itself to symbolizing this variety of possible approaches: the emblem of pure childish enjoyment of sugary sweetness, it can also be the object of mindful adult appreciation for the bitter taste of cocoa. Even alcoholic beverages can express the same duplicity in an adult context. As a matter of fact, Amélie rejoices when she discovers the matrix of alcohol: sugar. "Alcohol was the apotheosis of sugar, the proof of its divinity, the supreme moment of its life. Plum brandy was syrup that went to your head: it was the best thing in the world" (29). In certain contexts, the access to food exclusively through pleasure can therefore be entirely legitimate, because it is the expression of needs and drives to be heeded and respected.

I have already stressed that naked pleasure is both historical and contextual. Let's go back to *The Character of Rain*, where the access to life by way of the indulgence in white chocolate is preceded by a story about Amélie's relationship with her mother. A few months earlier, the girl had come to refuse breast milk because her mother represented (as often happens in reality) the antithesis of the grandmother: the denial of pleasure, the prohibition of sugar. "My mother had her theories about sugar, which, she felt, was responsible for most of the world's ills" (Nothomb 2003, 28). Amélie's mother is an advocate of modern dietary rationality and associates the consumption of sugar and cakes with a wide spectrum of physical illnesses.

In this context, the radical overturn of the medieval motto *quod sapit nutrit* is at play: *good is bad for you.* In contrast with this ideology, the paternal grandmother takes us to a different paradigm, where a positive relationship with taste is possible, and this is mediated by hunger and by the energy of pleasure. Taste experiences of great intensity are not only legitimate but fully desirable. The strategy of changing hierarchical food values is, therefore, also accompanied by moments of socially libertarian and politically incorrect emancipation. These differences in approaching taste are also historical: in the biographies of chefs and gastronomes—both in literature and in real life—the topic of a "generation gap" looms large. Moreover, the caregivers offering a passionate access to food are often the grandparents. For example, in Muriel Barbery's best-selling *Gourmet Rhapsody*, the grandmother is the source of gustatory desire. In the novel, Monsieur Arthens, a well-known food critic, reveals that his skills hail from his grandmother's kitchen: "I think that my entire career sprang from the fumes and aromas that came from that kitchen and which filled me, as a child, with desire. I literally went mad with desire. People don't really know what desire is, true desire, when it hypnotizes you and takes hold of your entire soul, surrounds it utterly, in such a way that you become demented, possessed, ready to do anything for a tiny crumb, for a whiff of whatever is being concocted there beneath your nostrils, subjugated by the devil's own perfume!" (Barbery 2009, 40). We will meet Monsieur Arthens again.

PLEASURE, IMAGE, AND PATHOLOGY

The experience of pleasure is often associated with representations and always with images—both internally (mental images) and externally (gestures and language). The image is the mode in which pleasure as a sensory input takes shape: in other words, without images, the vital impulse and its immediate continuation as a hedonic drive would not have a sensorial existence or form. Describing her taste of *spéculoos*, the famous Belgian spice cookies (another aesthetic encounter that leads to "roars of pleasure"), Amélie lives and intensifies her enjoyment through a mirror. Seeing oneself in a mirror is a fusion of image and representation. The mirror reflects one's own body as another body, and, doing that, it makes one reflect on "being an image" of sensibility. Moreover, seeing oneself represented during the act of enjoyment is also a joy. Actually, a real mirror is not necessary. Any medium, like verbal or gestural language, works. Nothomb writes: "I . . . began to eat, studying my *reflection. I wanted to see myself* in a state of pleasure. What I saw on my face was the taste of Speculoos. It was a real spectacle. Just by looking at myself, I could detect all the different flavours: there was definitely something sweet, or else I wouldn't have looked so happy; the sugar must have been brown, judging by the characteristic agitation of my dimples. A lot of cinnamon, said my nose, wrinkled in delight. My gleaming eyes announced the colour of the other spices, as unknown as they were exciting. As to the presence of honey, how could anyone have doubted it, seeing how my lips twitched with ecstasy? . . . The sight of my exquisite pleasure served only to intensify it" (Nothomb 2006, 51). This narcissistic description—mirrors are the home of narcissism—borders on autovoyeurism. The representation of the self by way of the reflected image heightens the pleasure and allows an analytical exploration of the details, particularly of the face: mouth, nose, and eyes. In the context of such an experience of solipsistic pleasure, the mirror can have the same function as the grandmother in the previous examples, namely, that of a distributor of pleasure, and as God, as the gustatory intertwining between perceiver and object perceived. It is as if pleasure required a third party, an outside eye, or a reflected other: this gustatory relationship, in other words, is not dual but threefold. Beyond the autovoyeuristic radicalization of the mirror, however, every ordinary experience of pleasure points to this threefold relational frame. Naked pleasure emerges always from a relationship that requires a *medium* (even if it is only our bodies seen by others). At the same time, this mediation is accomplished and experienced in that specific manner that does not approach food armed with the awareness of knowledge, but rather awaits and receives it unarmed.

The experience of food, in general, is an experience that is expressed via a third party. To expand a question that we will take up again in the next chapter, it must be remembered here that eating is the convivial, sharable, and, therefore, maybe mimetic experience par excellence. This act of sharing stems from the original mutuality of mother/infant relationship (Dissanayake 2000), and today it seems also to have a basis in biology related to the discovery of mirror neurons and their operating in the areas of the brain responsible for emotions and pleasure. In relation to our subject, it seems that the study of certain phenomena such as the aversion to or the desire for certain foods well illustrates *emphatic* sharing based on the theory of mirror neurons (the observation of a particular action causes the activation of the same neurons in the observer). Some examples are the very common phenomena of mouthwatering or of repulsion, when we see someone eating a food we adore or making a grimace of disgust, or the contagious smiles between mother and child during feeding (a case that we will get to in this chapter), or better still, in another context, that of contagious yawning. The need to share taste—through representations, gestures, and language—is as much biological as cultural: deeply rooted in our evolution, conviviality, in its broadest sense (from the Latin *cum vivere*, "living together"), has grown so much that by now it is part of our aesthetic nature.

A long time ago, one of the most basic functions of taste was nociception. Evolutionary speaking, the primary goal of taste is, in fact, a safeguard against damaging and toxic substances that would be harmful to the body and therefore to survival. The relationship between taste, health, and disease is crucial for our relational aesthetics. Even though this relationship is immediately complicated by exceptions and variables (not all disgusting or repulsive foods are toxic—just think of certain tasteless poisons—and not everything pleasant-tasting is healthy), it provides taste with a constant correlation with the states of psychophysical well-being or the lack thereof in structures of increasing complexity. In contrast to what is generally assumed, finding pleasure in food is initially closely related to health (Halpern 2005). If the infant has the ability to want and appreciate the food she needs in terms of nutrition, with the entry into adulthood pleasure moves away from its biological matrix and adheres to processes independent of the nociceptive function (Gibson 1966; Auvrey and Spence 2007). A fine and at times ineffable line between normality and pathology distinguishes the sphere of adult gustatory pleasure.

Amélie Nothomb's fiction also contains elements of taste regarding physical appearance in relation to psychological discomfort and mental illness: fatness, obesity, skinniness, physical deformation, anorexia, and bulimia. In *The Life of Hunger*, Amélie's father is an elusive and bulimic gentleman, obsessed by hunger but unable to feel pleasure. In another novel, *The Stranger Next Door*, obesity becomes a couple's mental code. The Bernardins, with the abnormal weight of their huge, wasted bodies alone and without so much as a word, become the psychic predators of their new and unsuspecting neighbors, Emile and Julette. Yet the Bernardins live their physical deformity in different ways. While Palamedes draws no pleasure from food and hovers between annoyance and indifference—"Mr. Bernardin was all the more *empty* for being *fat*: because he was *fat*, he had more volume to contain his emptiness"—his wife Bernadette, "the cyst," loves to eat and eats with pleasure (Nothomb 1995). Bernadette is obese, but not bulimic, she eats with gusto, but without being refined. Without knowing anything about the food she eats, she enjoys it compulsively, with an approach that mirrors a serious mental disorder, even insanity. If we leave coded and diagnosable disorders such as anorexia, bulimia, and binge eating disorder aside, many people have an ambiguous relationship with the pleasure of eating and oscillate between euphoric lapses and feelings of guilt. This oscillation is a tangible sign of how the religious sense of sin often transmigrates to a prohibition of the pleasure of food: that *good is bad for you* is the dietary translation of the supposed equation between knowledge and suffering.

CRITICISM AND THE LOOK OF CHILDHOOD

What has emerged from the examples given so far is that access to food by way of naked pleasure denies any value or virtue to the morals of privation: "This obvious fact should finally be attested:

asceticism doesn't enrich the spirit. There is no virtue in deprivation" (Nothomb 2006, 126). Now, the paradigm of this emancipative pleasure corresponds to the beginning of every individual life:
childhood. Here, behavior and choices are guided by hedonic drives
before we become structured according to the educational and cultural matrix in which we are placed or that is intentionally chosen.
Starting with the pleasure of food means starting with what comes
first in terms of the human experience, but also with what should
never be removed and hidden. We should be open to accept the
occasional reemergence of childhood during successive phases of
growth. The mind-set that strengthens the bond with that condition is frequently to be found in food, in the voluntary abandon
to the pleasure of chocolate, of beer, of wine without knowing its
history, without knowing its origin, and without any connection
to its sources. Whenever the context allows it and requires it, this
approach accepts a "passive" relationship with the object: it can *invade*
through its weight, its flavor, and its texture—alcohol *as* alcohol, the
sweet *as* sweet, and so on—regardless of its social and cultural matrix.
The pleasure of food may of course also depend on other factors,
and for adults this is sometimes the case. The expectation of that
particular wine or dish, the memory we have of it, the place where we
eat it, and the person with whom we eat it are all involved.

If we take a look at taste through the eyes of the researcher, taste
of course is always a social construct, the outcome of a field of forces
that marks complex processes of identification and differentiation.
If we look at taste *from within*, the possibilities of experience and
the perceptions we can carve out of it are numerous, legitimate,
and justifiable, depending on needs and contexts. Understanding
this does not mean, however, concluding that all experiences are
just and legitimate per se. There may be cases of inappropriate-
ness, error, and inconsistency with respect to the ecological situation. Imagine being invited to dinner at a very important gourmet
restaurant, Grant Achatz's Alinea, for example, and, once there,
demanding a T-Bone steak because that is just what you felt like
eating. Your behavior would be inappropriate, off topic, entirely
wrong, as if you had asked for background music at a Led Zeppelin

concert. Moreover, it is important to point out that the reference to the context does not imply a rigidly regulatory function of the context itself. The context is not a static or transcendental given; rather, it is a dynamic interaction between forces, which can therefore be changed, leaving space for creativity and transformation. The pleasure of food is always ambivalent. It can express desire for growth as well as pathological degeneration. It may be the banner of established powers, but it can also have a critical function. In this respect, the idea of gastronomy as the arena for rare and exceptional experiences too often sympathizes with the bourgeois idea of taste as "good taste," associated with a dominant trend, in short—to put it in a slightly simplistic but effective way—with "aesthetic capitalism" (Assouly 2008) and with a certain standardization of taste. Taking the relationship between aesthetics and childhood as a starting point is a strategic step for promoting a new strategy for the whole gastronomic experience, reflecting both a deeper and more open, amateur, inclusive, and aware look.

Naked pleasure corresponds to an *almost* instantaneous perception, phenomenalized first and foremost with sight: a bar of white chocolate puts the child in touch with her intelligence and capacity for observation, and it is precisely the look reflected in the mirror that enhances the pleasure of the spice cookies for Amélie. Gustatory pleasure is always related to the ability to see: to see oneself and to be seen. Casting a look is selective perception and visual intelligence: "Sight, the very essence of life, first and foremost constitutes a rejection. Therefore, to live means to reject" (Nothomb 2003, 11). Just like sight, taste as perception, recognition, and appreciation is also a process of editing and continuous dynamic selection, a process that proceeds systematically by acquiring information from the elements that make up an environment: places, people, sounds, smells, colors, individual experiences, constraints, contingent psychophysical conditions, appetite, and, of course, the chemical and physical characteristics of the object that is being ingested (Gibson 1966). The stimuli of sight are also embedded in this process to complete a complex multisensory perception where, in the words of Gibson, entire perceptual systems interact.

Looking refers to the face. The face is one of the fundamental elements for understanding taste attitudes because—anticipated or *in vivo*—gustatory pleasure is expressed through facial gestures and words. In a pioneering study titled *Le doux et l'amer* (1985), the psychologist Matty Chiva presented the results of research on taste perception in infants. Chiva and his team analyzed the relationship between facial expression and perception of taste in infants through photographs taken during feeding. Babies responded with great pleasure to the taste of sugar and sweetness, were less excited about saltiness, and demonstrated disgust and repulsion to sour and bitter-tasting food. These responses—a smile or a grimace of disgust—were photographed and catalogued. In addition, another element emerged, which attracted the attention of researchers: the relationship between mother and infant. Chiva and his team noticed that in the presence of the mother infants tend to replicate maternal facial expressions. Later, from the age of about a year and a half onward, they intentionally and explicitly communicate their emotional states using facial expressions associated with taste. The pleasure of food substantiated in the face is therefore the fundamental way toward expressing emotions, but it is also the first way to create relations with the external world. The careful observation of these phenomena helps pinpoint the development between nature and culture in the dynamic and adaptive picture of the human process. The scene in which such emotional mimicry takes place, in other words, is emotionally and socially characterized from the outset. The infant's facial expression begins to *signify* something through her relationship with her mother; through this process, the dynamic and differential metamorphosis from biological to cultural occurs (Chiva 1985, 40–85). How is it possible then to underestimate this kind of gustatory pleasure? The famous Italian chef Fulvio Pierangelini once said that the most profound aim of cooking—that of pleasing people—is a very difficult thing to achieve, because it actually means trying to improve on that most intimate and inaugural act of childhood: breastfeeding.

Other issues derive from these considerations about the mimicry of pleasure and the ongoing link between nature and culture: the relationship between anthropological constants and cultural variations, as well as, more generally, between animality and humanity. As is well known, even Charles Darwin addressed the question of the face—though not in relation to taste—in *The Expression of the Emotions in Man and Animals* (1872), comparing the facial expressions of babies with those of animals. Darwin concluded that interspecies facial expressions had much in common. His theories were very important also for evolutionary aesthetics, although not in the field of food. Studies examining expressions of pleasure or disgust for food in infants, however, illuminate the interaction between the physiological, psychological, and social levels of the sensory experience. This constant interaction continues into adulthood and is the basis for individual skills and techniques in many fields of human existence. What is relevant here is that during human growth, the social level tends to cover and engulf the other two. In particular, physiological and biological elements are apparently removed, regardless of the fact that the link between all levels is the key to growth. Culture, which appears to us as the result of one single dimension, thus becomes impoverished. Gustatory taste is no exception to this mechanism, and thus asserting the importance of naked pleasure entails, in an only apparently paradoxical fashion, doing justice to the complexity of culture. There are, of course, good reasons for this shift in manners from childhood to adulthood: one's upbringing is preparation for a social life and should above all provide tools for critical thought. Very often infantile gustatory pleasure is a tool for manipulation to keep people in a perpetual "minority status," to use a Kantian expression. *Junk food* is an emblematic case of the degeneration of the vital hedonic impulse in commercial manipulation, which is why one sees adults continuing to eat like children *in every respect*, including attraction to the same foods, the sweet and the soft. This is an indisputable fact. Cultural evolution and the channeling of impulses into paths more appropriate to socialization are good. Fundamental attention, however, has to be paid to avoiding their complete removal, because removal has dangerous and serious consequences. In the realm of food and taste, allow me to mention one point I will develop in the next chapter: the axiological distinction between nutrition (the sphere of the primary, energetic need) and cuisine (the sphere of desire, imagination, and creativity) loses its plausibility. In fact, eating is not a purely quantitative action, and pleasure is not a luxury typical of rich and postindustrial societies. This is a curious myth, because it is a fact that pleasure grows with the intensity of the appetite. Unfortunately, this misunderstanding influences some contemporary expressions of gastronomic culture: great chefs who think they ought to be appreciated not for the physical and nutritional value of their food, but for the intellectual pleasure they provide—even implying that it's best to go to the best restaurants "without being hungry" in order to better appreciate the food—find themselves, against their will, in a counterintuitive and counterproductive cul-de-sac. Instead, an aesthetics of taste as ecological relationship, since it appraises naked pleasure, is also an aesthetics of hunger. To subscribe to this position, it is enough to observe and to observe oneself, honestly and in line with one's psychophysical processes, inextricably comprising reason and passion, ideas and feelings. We need to do away with the accretions that encumber our feelings. Of course, this is not a matter of rediscovering a naive naturalism, let alone believing in the absolute spontaneity of feelings. Instead, the reevaluation of naked childhood pleasure—which may be defined as the *nonintentional* childhood look—must be heeded as a warning against all hypostatized dichotomies.

Pleasure as Nature in Culture

The naked pleasure of food, testified by the need and desire for raw tastes, hunger, and pure delight, is an aesthetic value that emerges from a complex and multifaceted network of experiences and relationships. According to our pragmatic and relational aesthetics, such an aesthetic value reveals the link between the two opposite poles of nature and culture. Pleasure is needed for enjoyment and, at the same time, enjoyment of a necessity. Naked pleasure is a perceptual experience driven by impulses and needs that are not governed by conscious intentions. Moving toward more complex cognitive levels—those of the adult world—pleasure gets dressed, becoming codified, and taste becomes specified. In other words, we can define taste as culture. In the context of adulthood, the occurrence of naked pleasure will express a different need, that of the recuperation of a previous level of experience. Following the Vichian idea of the recurring cycle, we can perceive in this idea the resurgence of nature in culture.

Many years ago, a famous wine producer told me a story. He was convinced that "good" was a universally appreciable category and to test his hypothesis he conducted a little experiment. A lover of great French wines, he took a few bottles of a famous *premier cru* Bordeaux, poured it into plain bottles—the same ones used at the company cafeteria—and served it to his employees. According to him, the result was unequivocal: everyone noticed a big difference in the wine and appreciated the novelty, even asking him for more over the next few days. The people unknowingly involved in the manufacturer's experiment had experienced adult pleasure, "directly" without a safety net. Beyond the actual veracity of this story, the anecdote is significant because it allows us to formulate a question for further exploring the relationship between nature and culture. Is gustatory pleasure universally perceivable? The point here is twofold. On the one hand, we need to ask the question as to whether it is necessary to have certain skills (as was said in the eighteenth century, "good taste") in order to experience a *sensorial* pleasure. The wine producer's experiment aimed at showing that enjoyment can also be experienced by people with no special knowledge of that object, or rather at demolishing the opposite theory, namely, that skills and culture are necessary in order to appreciate the good (or the beautiful). The problem, however, is that this example pertains to wine, an object strongly characterized in adult and cultural terms (there are societies that do not drink wine, or only drink wine marginally, though it seems that wine is becoming more and more globalized). And I assume that quite different questions arise with chocolate or other less specific and more elementary foods. Wine is usually taken as a paradigm for gastronomic expertise, but to what extent can we totally accept this assumption? Even if cultural knowledge is important for the appreciation of artifacts—apart from discussions here about the nature of such artifacts as wine—the question is whether *aesthetic* pleasure as naked enjoyment is possible *from the perspective of the perceiver*, before knowledge of any sort. This is a central issue in the history of modern aesthetics: let's have a look at two key moments.

The French philosopher Jean-Baptiste Dubos in his *Critical Reflections on Poetry, Painting and Music* (originally published in France in 1719) offered an interesting answer: "Do we ever reason, in order to know whether a ragoo be good or bad; and has it ever entered into any body's head, after having settled the geometrical principles of taste, and defined the qualities of each ingredient that enters into the composition of those messes, to examine into the proportion observed in their mixture, in order to decide whether it be good or bad? No, this is never practiced. We have a sense given us by nature to distinguish whether the cook acted according to the rules of his art. People taste the ragoo, and tho' unacquainted with those rules, they are able to tell whether it be good or no" (Dubos 1748, 2:238–39). According to Dubos, the perception of pleasure but *at the same time* what is needed for the appreciation of the quality of an artifact and an artwork cannot be reduced to rational analysis or the culture possessed by the observer, and the gustatory pleasure of food falls within this framework. Dubos, one of the founders of the "aesthetics of the beholder" (that is, of aesthetics that consider the public's judgment as central to the qualitative evaluation of a work), uses ragout as an example. In fact, for Dubos, taste—both a bodily sense and an immaterial and vague capability—enables us to orient ourselves in aesthetic evaluations, and to recognize and appreciate the good and the beautiful. If we assume that Dubos is right, and if then aesthetic *judgment* ("this is a good ragout") does not depend on the previous knowledge of rules, a fortiori this will hold for aesthetic *pleasure*. This is why such a pleasure may de jure be experienced by everyone. The argument, though, does not imply that naked pleasure is without context. Interpersonal relationships, family imprinting, individual style, and the specific environment in which an experience takes place produce specific differences that explain both agreements and disagreements over gustatory perceptions. Nor does the theme ignore the difference, in terms of intensity and awareness, between the experiences of pleasure undergone by skilled or ignorant persons. Perhaps Dubos's position corrects the wine producer's radical approach that is so difficult to wholly support: if, theoretically, a pleasure can be experienced by all, this, in fact, is not always the case. This correction brings us closer to the thesis of the aesthetics of taste as experience and relationship.

Kant's position on this topic was, however, very different, and it contributed greatly to the exclusion of gustatory pleasure, seen as merely sensual (from which "naked" can be seen in a pejorative sense), from the aesthetic domain. According to Kant, there is a radical difference between sensual gustatory enjoyment and aesthetic pleasure. The first is individual, private, and not universal, while the second refers to a common and universal human feeling. The pleasures of eating fall into the first domain because gustatory taste refers only to the physical senses, biological necessity, and human need. Kant rejected Dubos's and other's approach to aesthetics because of their lack of transcendental rigor. Kant's brilliantly famous and very influential move was in fact to introduce a new specific faculty to explain those aesthetic emotions, feelings, and judgments, which did not correspond either to sensitivity or to the intellect, and which he called "power of judgment" (*Urteilskraft*). According to Kant, aesthetic perception is neither intellectual nor even purely sensitive or emotional. Food pleasure then belongs only to this second domain and is quite distinct from the human desire for beauty and from its universal appreciation. Today, it is easy to object to Kant's aesthetics with respect to the distinction he drew between sensual enjoyment and aesthetic pleasure, as well as that between agreeable and beautiful. Instead of making technical philosophical arguments (Korsmeyer 1999), however, I would rather focus our attention on simple observation. On the one hand, the appreciation for a food or a drink could be driven by a perception comprising specific skills able to distinguish pleasantness from other qualities (we will get to this issue in the next chapter). On the other hand, an infant's enjoyment while sucking at her mother's breast is a necessary and universal pleasure, just as (or perhaps more than) the pleasure derived from a landscape or a work of art. Gustatory pleasure can be an aesthetic pleasure therefore, even if it has different characteristics from visual or auditory pleasure. In the prevalent epistemological and aesthetic model of Western thought, a big obstacle consists in assuming, explicitly or otherwise, that visual perception is the unique paradigm, while contact senses remain marginalized or excluded.

My suggestion is that there is no irreversible route leading from naked pleasure to dressed taste, but rather a continuous and dynamic interaction. With this idea, we can overcome barriers between enjoyment and appreciation, between sensitive pleasure and aesthetic pleasure, and between nature and culture in a pragmatic fashion. Let's go back then to wine, and once more consider the question of its possible appreciation in terms of pleasure without culture. Wine tasting is, in fact, often seen as the paradigm of expertise, a skill acquired over time through practice. It is much more common to meet someone purporting to "understand nothing" about wine, and with no knowledge of how to appreciate it, than it is to meet someone who makes the same claim about food. We have all eaten since birth, every day, but the same can't be said for alcohol consumption, which is voluntary and adult consumption par excellence, and in particular for wine, which is not only alcohol but one of its more particular elaborations. However, in this case too, daily observation shows us that taste experiences are differently situated, growing and developing in different theaters of meaning and in different contexts. In some cases, perceptual experience without prior knowledge or specific cultural equipment is perfectly legitimate and can provide the highest aesthetic pleasure. The example of the winemaker who wanted his employees to enjoy a great wine without mediation is part of a very large case record that anyone can substantiate by him- or herself: uninitiated people can easily enjoy and appreciate complex wines. Moreover, this experience of pleasure can also affect those who possess taste skill in order to transit between naked pleasure and dressed taste. Sometimes these two levels are conflicting: we like something that for ethical or political reasons we should not like or, on the contrary, for the same reasons we do not like something that we should like. In other words, quite often, our gustatory perception proposes experiences and relationships that, if carefully considered, take us back to a plea-sure we cannot *justify* on the basis of theoretical or cultural reasoning, referring us, rather, back to our primordial past.

THE ETHICS OF PLEASURE: GOOD THAT DOES "GOOD"

The liberating value of pleasure that we have observed in the nov-els of Amélie Nothomb can be lived in everyday life as an ethical program. In one sentence: good does us "good," and what does us "good" does everyone else "good" too. In opposition to the religious and ethical condemnation of sensorial pleasure stands the idea that pleasure contributes to the welfare and happiness not only of a single individual, but also of society and humankind at large. The para-digm that, reversing the hierarchy of the senses, establishes duty in pleasure is in Epicurus's thought or—more correctly—in its popular diffusion. Epicurus is regarded as the "gourmets' philosopher" par excellence, and in everyday language, "epicurean" has become synon-ymous with gourmet and gourmand, or simply someone who enjoys the pleasures of life. Although the philosophy of Epicurus is more complex than its vulgarization (Symons, 2007, and also the fourth chapter of this book, where I will deal with Epicurus again), it is use-ful to emphasize a position that, throughout the history of Western thought, was a constant thorn in the Platonic side.

"The beginning and root of every good is the pleasure of the stom-ach. Even wisdom and the refinements are referable to this" (Athe-naeus of Naukratis 1929, II A.D., 12, pp. 546–47). This extraordinary aphorism, attributed to Epicurus, is from *The Deipnosophists* (which translates as "Philosophers at Dinner" or "The Gastronomes") by Athenaeus, the great writer from Naukratis who lived around the second century AD. In *The Deipnosophists*, the term *gastronomy* is also documented for first time, in reference to a lost book by Archestra-tus of Gela. Whether Epicurus actually did or did not express this thought, its content is of great theoretical importance for an aesthet-ics of taste as experience. The physical pleasure of the stomach is the *beginning* and *root* of every good: the material enjoyment of food is the original root of the good, intended as an ethics of happiness. As is common knowledge, in ancient Western philosophy aesthetics and ethics are often related, even if their go-between is, of course, not food but beauty. The Latin language also bears witness to this relationship: the adjective *beautiful* (*bellum*) derives from *good* (*bonum*), by way of the diminutive *bonellum* (Tatarkiewicz 1980). For this reason, the thought attributed to Epicurus is important for an ethics of pleasure. The link between good as (gustatory) pleasure and the good—the ultimate goal of human life, what makes life worth living, and what corresponds to happiness in Epicurus's philosophy—is the manifesto for a new way of living.

The bond between aesthetics and ethics has been proposed again in various ways and by many authors in the course of Western modern history. In the twentieth century, for example, Ludwig Wittgenstein stated that "ethics and aesthetics are one." But there are more radical positions, ones that emphasize the supremacy of aesthetics over ethics: just think of the famous axiom expressed by Prince Myshkin in Dostoyevsky's *The Idiot*: "Beauty will save the world." Or think of the theory of the psychologist James Hillman on the "politics of beauty," namely, that effective political action starts with the reappropriation of the ability to perceive, and to reject the bad, the degraded, and the discordant (Hillman 2006). Or, again, think of the artistic practice of Joseph Beuys, the goal of which was to demonstrate that every human being is an artist, suggesting that aesthetics be regarded with the perspective of everyday practices aiming to influence and to change the world around us. One may even think of Joseph Brodsky's surprising observation in his acceptance speech on the occasion of the award of the Nobel Prize for Literature in 1987, when he said that "aesthetics is the mother of ethics." The most plausible meaning of Brodsky's daring declaration is that at the foundation of ethical behavior, the good in an ethical sense, lies its desirability and the satisfaction we receive from pursuing such behavior. The pleasure of acting one way rather than another marks the true ethical agent (Eaton Muelder 1997). One might even claim that aesthetic desires establish the rational values that make up the sphere of ethics—or, less radically, that rational values and aesthetic values, reasons and imagination, are intertwined from the very beginning. As the philosopher Cora Diamond maintains, an ethical imagination awakens the sense of our humanity—meaning agreement on that systemic and evolutionary concept of aesthetics that has led us to consider nature and culture as jointly liable elements and two sides of the same coin. How can such a view exclude taste perception from its consideration? How can the fundamental question regarding the origins of a sense of beauty not also imply the theme of the origin of the sense of the good and, with it, of gustatory pleasure?

Of course, the attribution of a fundamental emancipatory value to the body is not a new theme in Western thought, as philosophers such as Spinoza, Merleau-Ponty, and others have reminded us. It becomes more difficult, however, to find someone who speaks for the body as gustatory pleasure. Among them, we can mention Feuerbach (to whom we will return in the third chapter), Nietzsche, Charles Fourier (Brillat-Savarin's cousin, who dedicated a few pages of his *Theory of the Four Movements and the General Destinies* to gastronomy as a virtuous synthesis of harmony and social welfare; Fourier 1996), and the aforementioned Emmanuel Lévinas. From their own perspective, each of these authors emphasizes the importance of a philosophy with or through food. They argue that gustatory pleasure is not opposed to knowledge as subjective and idiosyncratic, and that it is not foreign to aesthetics, despite being both physical and ephemeral. Nor does it represent a danger to ethical thought inasmuch as it is egotistical and uncontrollable. Instead, gustatory pleasure is valued *precisely because* it allows the rejection of a paradigm of knowledge, of aesthetics, and of ethics in which one does not want to recognize oneself anymore. However, to recover the radicalism of the verdict attributed to Epicurus, it might be necessary to look beyond philosophy. In literature, maybe Epicurus's successor can be considered François Rabelais, the author of *The Life of Gargantua and Pantagruel*, the novel of the body and the pleasures of food par excellence, in which the universe and all its relations are explored through the lens of food consumption.

Is it possible to find attitudes consistent with the consequences of Epicurus's thought in real life? Can we see the tracks of our own relational existence in the pleasure of food and extrapolate our adhesion to our social ties? Here we need to bring different ways to bear on this issue. Let's take, for example, the famous movie *Babette's Feast*. This story proposes a solution, but within a context that upholds social values strengthened by religious faith. The pleasure of food is designed to place these values in a new and renewed light. Babette, through the pleasure bestowed upon the ignorant villagers (a variation of the scene of the grandmother administering chocolate to Amélie), manages to kindle a *sensus communis*, a universal and communal feeling that had been hidden by disembodied precepts and rules. If we wanted to answer this question in purely immanent terms, the answer would have less obvious exemplars. Fourier, for instance, who tried to theorize a social system based on free love and gastronomic pleasures, was a utopian and a visionary. In the fourth chapter of this essay, I will offer a broader interpretation of Epicurus's thought and will attempt to propose a plausible, comprehensible, and mindful attitude of considering sensual pleasure. The difficulty in answering the above question leads us directly to the second modality for accessing taste: taste as knowledge and culture, in its *dressed* taste.

The path of naked pleasure is the main and primary access to food. The variations of the human being (in both ontogenic and phylogenetic terms) must not remove or hinder it. In adulthood, it is the necessary allusion to the biological and instinctual depths that constitutes our human nature. "Nature" here does not imply naturalism; nature pinpoints a *prereflexive ingenuity*, as the one that characterizes an infant's gaze: the relationship with the environment prior to reflection. In the course of one's life, this is also an irreplaceable imprint, the sign of everyone's unique individuality. It is universal as a need or desire and is singular as it is differentiated with respect to the different environments and situations in which it has developed. Naked gustatory pleasure can be a valuable, free, primitive, and regenerating endowment. If properly understood, it can also be a powerful tool of resistance against dominant and hegemonic discourses on taste, made by the dominant class (Bourdieu 1984). Just as irony corrodes the seriousness of philosophical discourse and candid vulgarity bothers culture, bare pleasure buzzes around knowledge and sometimes manages to challenge it. However, growth marks its steps. The infant grows into an adult. Nude pleasure gets dressed, imbuing itself with new layers of meaning and with sharing and negotiating. Imagine experts or enthusiastic foodies discussing a dish: if the criterion of discussion and appreciation were set exclusively on naked pleasure, the dispute would stop immediately. It is precisely this *impasse* to which the famous medieval motto "de gustibus non est disputandum" refers, because taste as an expression of individual and naked pleasure cannot form the basis for a negotiation. Instead, in a discussion among experts or foodies the appreciation for a dish or a drink is rightly and inevitably expressed through a shared grammar based on common elements, beyond the dimension of pleasure, toward an idea of quality. This fluid, dynamic difference between two levels of taste experience—naked pleasure and dressed taste—marks the thin line between the first and the second access to eating.

Second Mode of Access

Knowledge

> *I have enjoyed peaches and apricots more since I have known that they were first cultivated in China in the early days of Han Dynasty; that Chinese hostages held by the great King Kaniska introduced them to India, whence they spread to Persia, reaching the Roman Empire in the first century of our era; that the word "apricot" is derived from the same Latin source as the word "precocious," because the apricot ripens early; and that the A at the beginning was added by mistake, owing to a false etymology. All this makes the fruit taste much sweeter.*
> — BERTRAND RUSSELL

The second way to taste conceives of taste as knowledge and aware-ness of culture. In this perceptual experience, taste operates as the conscious fabric of a person's biographical and cultural identity, a progressive acquisition. Here taste is "dressed," controlled, and ded-icated to appreciation as the capacity of understanding over time. Calling this experience "taste" does not connote the predominance of a hedonic impulse but that of reason, reflection, and balance. There are many ramifications along this mode of access to taste because, unlike the experience of naked pleasure, which tends to lack the capacity to reflect and is therefore less articulated, it develops on many different levels of awareness—from the novice's curiosity to the most sophisticated *connoisseur's* expertise—and it provides many consequent options. The curious person, the enthusiast, the *gourmet* but also health fanatics and vegetarians fall into this category because they all express a gustatory appreciation from *qualitative* and *esteem-ing* criteria that arrange an aesthetic judgment. If naked pleasure is basically the realm of unreflected and often *tacit* desire, dressed taste is the land of *explicit*, conceptualized, and often verbosely expressed knowledge. Please note that I am not proposing again here a dichotomy that I aimed to deconstruct before (desire/knowledge, nature/culture, and the like)! Instead, I propose to observe different modes of experiencing food from the perceiver's perspective, as I have previously noted, *from inside* the perception. To give examples that have already been discussed, wine in this case will not be appreciated simply *as* "wine" or alcohol, or chocolate *as a* generic sweet or sugar bearer. Rather, particular wines or chocolates will convey constitutive values of appreciation through taste. Gustatory perception is consciously oriented toward such an exploration in order to obtain pleasure intensified by knowledge and culture or modeled on it in a sort of intellectual enjoyment. However, expertise is not always necessary for dressed taste: its domain is not only about recognition and awareness of one's identity but also just as much about the approximation to otherness and exoticism. A plate of *tortellini* or *arancini* can be appreciated because of the memories they stir, fried grasshoppers can be appreciated because they are exotic, Sauternes can be appreciated because of its nobility and its production method. Connection to the past, open-mindedness, and broadening cultural perspectives are all ways in which the subject, armed with projects, horizons of expectation, and particular interpretative schemes, approaches the object on a scale that ranges from primary, basic curiosity to the most sophisticated connoisseurship.

LEARNING ABOUT QUALITY, CULTIVATING TASTE

My experience as a teacher and wine taster, an activity I have practiced for several years at a professional level, has taught me a good deal about the development of learning and cultivating taste. Using my personal background, I will now start to sketch some lines that can be useful for understanding a number of basic processes regarding the access to food via dressed taste. My skills were clearly formed through practice (tasting many different wines, building an archive for the recognition of some recurring features, and making comparisons as a habit), study (reading books and journals, keeping up to date on new products, and so on), and trips to vineyards, wineries, and meetings with producers and winemakers at their places and at fairs and events. During this apprenticeship, I was "promoted" to taster and educator of the tastes of others. The quotation marks are there because there is no "school of taste," there is no institution certifying that someone has "good taste" for wine or food, just as there is no school that guarantees a degree in good criticism or—to look at the issue from the side not of judging, but rather of making—no school one can graduate from as a good writer. This impossibility is most revealing; neither the fields of taste and criticism nor the fields of creating artworks or artifacts are subject to general and abstractly computable certifications. There are of course schools of tasting and sensory training, as well as those of literary criticism, journalism, and creative writing, but they provide the basic tools for understanding the backbone of the functioning of these activities. Success—becoming a *good* critic, a *good* taster, or a *good* artist—is an entirely different story. That is up to individual talent, to a personal process and development of something that is recognized *as good*. Such evaluation is made ex post by the same communities of affiliation—the critics, the tasters, the artists—and by the public, the general audience (Shapin 2012).

As a wine-tasting teacher, I have taught many courses for both beginners and advanced students who in vivo helped me to understand the difference between the expression of individual naked and immediate pleasure and qualitative evaluation. Educating taste aims first at teaching words, a grammar, and a syntax of quality that express a reasoned appreciation of what is ingested and assimilated (Smith 2007). This process develops through various stages. At the first step, the beginner acquires the tools for building a value-oriented reference system. But how does this acquisition occur? Instead of "acquisition"—a word that underlies the idea of gathering knowledge as it was "already given"—it would be more correct to speak of interaction, active correspondence, and negotiation (Ingold 2013). In fact, masters are the authorities that teach a system of values. They provide examples and, thanks to their persuasive and seductive ability (*seduce* comes from the Latin *se ducere*, "to lead a person toward oneself"), convince the novices of the "truth" of the system proposed. The language of taste here is under construction. Let me give a personal example: Many years ago, I wanted to verify a particular fact about this process. In an introductory wine-tasting class, I proposed to focus on quality in wine through concepts and perceptions expressed by words like *flavor* and *acidity*. Was it a neutral gesture? Clearly not, because from those features I stressed a certain idea of quality based on values like drinkability, elegance, lightness. I recommended a whole language of wine, which depended on that initial move and convinced others through *gestures*, *postures*, and *facial expressions* that a quality wine had to have exactly those characteristics.

Before finishing my direct evidence, let me offer an important clarification. Around the middle of the twentieth century, the distinction between so called nonaesthetic properties and aesthetic properties (or qualities) was introduced into aesthetics to explain how qualitative values are established in works of art. In short, the nonaesthetic properties correspond to the characteristics that define an object or work of art in physicochemical and quantitative terms. These properties are easily discernible and measurable: color, shape, weight, volume, and composition. Aesthetic properties, on the other hand, are those attributions that involve a very problematic area, namely, that domain of qualitative perception called *aesthetic perception* where properties such as harmony, finesse, elegance, appeal, and balance are taken into consideration (Sibley 2007). Now the problem is to discover whether there is some kind of a relationship between the aesthetic and the nonaesthetic properties. If so, what is it? Without entering into the merit of the many possible answers offered by scholars, I would only like to point out that the question applies perfectly to our case as well. In the tasting course, in fact, I wanted to convince the students that flavor and acidity—nonaesthetic properties, subject to measurement and quantitative analysis—were *closely linked* to certain aesthetic properties such as drinkability, lightness, and elegance. Now that this has been made clear, and keeping it in mind, I can conclude my story. In another introductory course with a different group of novices, I proposed focusing on quality in wine through completely different concepts and perceptions, expressed by nonaesthetic properties such as alcohol content, fruitiness, and sweetness. I then connected these properties to the *same* aesthetic properties of the previous course: drinkability, elegance, and appeal. In both courses, I obviously justified my value system, not only by way of seductive and rhetorical strategies, but also with reasonable arguments taken from wine production. With an audience of beginners, in two "experimental" courses, I obtained the same outcome—a good measure of pleasure and new wine enthusiasts—by constructing two diverse and in a certain way opposite paradigms of taste as value and qualitative appraisal.

My little experiment is not supposed to suggest a skeptical conception of taste. I do not intend to argue that taste is just a matter of private preferences in the line of "de gustibus non est disputandum." This *motto* refers to taste as naked and immediate pleasure, to instances where impulses encounter flavors, that terrain where the gustatory perception exhibits our *uniqueness*, our unwavering signature. Taste cannot be *discussed* here, it can only be reported. This is a good thing, as we argued in the first chapter; there are aesthetic encounters that need to be seen in this light. From a different angle, however, taste is the chosen topic of discussion, a true "social negotiating table." We are also social and often sociable beings. For this reason, dressed taste is what is most debated and demands criteria, values, and judgment. It requires knowledge and culture, shared through socially coded patterns of behavior and a corresponding grammar. The example of the wine-tasting courses helps us understand how *aesthetic* knowledge concerning aesthetic properties comes about through negotiation, a comparison of perspectives that does not have a *causal* foundation, but instead contingent motivations and hence historical, anthropological, and social ones. Harmony and elegance, beauty and finesse, personality and character are *not* caused by a wine's physicochemical components; rather, they depend on them in a different way. They are perceived by virtue of specific training that produces an ability to perceive the second degree, diverse from standard perception, which is therefore defined as taste. Taste is the mark of aesthetic perception (Levinson 2005). Aesthetic perception, however, is not a definitive and fixed stage. It changes and develops in accordance with the historical significance of the values it captures, but also with respect to every single experience and environment in which it occurs. If the first gustatory aesthetic relationship we have analyzed in terms of naked pleasure corresponds to the vital impulse and delight, in the transition toward cognitive and cultural stages aesthetic appreciation becomes even more specialized and articulated.

The historicity of gustatory aesthetic perception affects both individuals—tastes change, and they change because experiences, perspectives, and more generally the values attributed to objects change—and society as a whole. The values associated with wine substantiate this well. My personal experiment showed two different systems at play, one typical of the 1990s, according to which wine had to be structured, dense, soft, and fruity, the other, which is currently popular, according to which wine has to be crispy, light, fresh, and mineral. Those novices and unwitting victims of my basic tests, who continued to broaden their knowledge and developed a greater tasting capacity, might have begun to harbor certain doubts about the paradigm imparted by me in retrospect. Maybe someone has transformed their initial curiosity into true *expertise*, and in this process their perceptual amelioration, their ability for discernment and judgment, has increased. With those former students, I can no longer draw up grids of value to my liking, but instead I would have to face them and negotiate as between peers.

If education and training play a crucial role in the constitution of adult gustatory perception and are the way toward dressed taste, it is furthermore impossible to ignore the basic conditionings that structure our perception, an involuntary legacy that cannot be done away with. Explicit projects and conscious purposes to establish one's style and identity are one thing; the background of individual biographies, memories and social environment in which one has grown up and been raised are another (Auvrey and Spence 2007; Burnham and Skilleås 2012). In the example above, the project that the beginners chose by enrolling in the wine course was to learn a perceptual ability and the appropriate language skills to describe a sensory perception and its subsequent qualitative assessment. This is normally what people attending a wine-tasting class expect, but since I happened to be their teacher, I gave them something more to learn, aesthetic perception. In fact, I have been arguing that taste perception comprises two different levels, sensory perception and aesthetic perception. This assumption needs to be discussed since it is controversial.

According to a certain view—shared, for example, by some sensory chemists and analysts who are more in tune with the "hard" sciences and statistics than with philosophy and the humanities (Noble 2006)—the only possible and "objective" gustatory perception is standard perception. This perception, as we said above, refers only to nonaesthetic properties such as the levels of acidity and tannins as well as the presence of certain aromas rather than others. In this context, training taste would mean learning to perceive, recognize, and appreciate standard characteristics, similarly to what occurs when a child learns to recognize colors and shapes of objects and the letters of the alphabet. In this conception, beyond standard perception, taste "non est disputandum." The defenders of such a position claim it is the only reasonable way to discuss and to share judgments about food and wine. On the contrary, they argue that adjectives such as *harmonious*, *elegant*, and *vibrant* would express only individual preferences. Words such as *balance*, *finesse*, *power*, or *grace* would not denote anything real and would only correspond to pure personal idiosyncrasies, exempt from any reference to the tasted object. It is easy to refute this concept. First, it works with the subject/object paradigm that we already put into question, replacing it with the relational and ecological paradigm. According to the latter, taste perception is a complex skill, aimed at different purposes and projects. In this framework, recognizing quality is recognizing values rather than mere facts, as the former paradigm would affirm. In other words, we are freer. It is entirely legitimate, and for some purposes even useful, to enhance the sensory practice of flavor and aroma recognition by training taste and smell aesthetically, as these senses are generally underestimated and therefore not used to the fullest of their capacities. But—and this is the second point—this does not imply that standard gustatory perception (flavors "as such," aromas "as such") is neutral and not itself biased. It's just another game, as has been argued also by historians and social scientists (Perullo 2012b; Shapin 2011). Third, sensory perception does not cover everything that taste allows one to do: it is perfectly possible to distinguish between two wines with a similar sensory profile but dissimilar final qualities, different values. Think of the different prices of two wines belonging to two adjacent but diverse vineyards that cannot be explained just by sensory features. If the price differential is warranted, it calls for other arguments, both perceptual—standard and aesthetic—perceptual and nonperceptual. These arguments compose the domain of aesthetic. Aesthetic sensibility is the capacity to ecologically correspond to the intertwining of facts and values; it does not pertain to the complexity of the reasons that temporarily and historically justify certain value orientations. Learning about quality and cultivating taste, therefore, means facing our inescapable relationship with food, making it an integral part of our experiences. It also means consciously exercising one's perceptive ability in the direction of the complexity of embodied knowledge, leaving the environment around us to interact with our psychophysical system.

TASTING THE WORLD

Experiencing food while traveling is one of the most deliberate, appreciated, and popular ways of approaching the culture of new and unusual places. Wine and food tourism is on the rise, in particular with regard to the aesthetics of traditions and their territories. The encounter with "other" food in contexts differing from the usual ones is also an extremely rich topos, from Montaigne to Stevenson, from Twain to Chatwin. The travel writer John Foster Fraser describes the discovery of a fish in Burma in his book *Round the World on a Wheel* (1989), which narrates a bicycle trip that lasted over two years: "We investigated how the food was prepared. First of all the fish were caught and laid in the sun for three days to dry. The fish being then dead, though moving, were pounded in plenty of salt. Then they were put into a jar, and when the mouth was opened people five miles away knew all about it. *Nga-pee*, I soon saw, was a delicacy that could only be appreciated by cultured palates. The taste is original; it is salt, rather like rancid butter flavoured with Limburger cheese, garlic, and paraffin oil. The odor is more interesting than the taste. It is more conspicuous" (265). This passage makes clear how taste can serve as an *active probe* for the discovery of the world, in direct experience as well as in academic research: much of *cultural studies* today is about food as a marker for multicultural complexity (Counihan and Van Esterik 1997).

In a well-known story originally published 1982 with the title *Sapore Sapere* (Taste Knowledge) (which in 1986 was changed to *Under the Jaguar Sun*), Italo Calvino described some itineraries of taste as knowledge and culture in great depth. In the Italian edition, the story opens with a long epigraph from Niccolò Tommaseo's *Dizionario dei sinonimi*,[1] which provides further clarification about the original meaning of taste. This is what the Italian linguist wrote in his famous work published in 1830: "*Tasting*, in general, exercising the sense of taste, receiving its impression, even without a deliberate will or without thought. The sampling becomes more determined in order to taste and to know what one is tasting; or at least it denotes that from the first impression comes a reflected sentiment, an idea, the beginning of an experience. Therefore, to the Latins, *sapio* in translation meant feeling correctly; and therefore the sense of the Italian *sapere* [to know], which in itself stands for the right doctrine and for the prevailing of knowledge over science" (Calvino 1988, 23). Tommaseo distinguished between a direct impression, before any intention and reflection, and a reflective exploration, aimed at recognition and intellectual appreciation. Then he referred to the etymology of the Italian verb *sapere* (to know), from the Latin *sapio* (originally "to have taste" and, by extension, "to know"). Tasting, therefore, means correctly perceiving a substance's immediate taste, but also its subsequent recognition following an investigation. According to Tommaseo, taste is a double ability, related to the same double nature and meaning of the *sense*. This word in fact denotes both the immediate sensation (the instant "epidermal" sensation) and good sense ("to have good sense"), something that helps us choose and orient ourselves. A few decades before Tommaseo, the French gastronome

Jean Anthelme Brillat-Savarin had already offered a similar and even more precise definition of taste. According to him, taste is a combination of three elements corresponding to three consecutive steps: *direct* sensation (the immediate introduction of a food item into the mouth, with the activation of all receptors responsible for the recognition of chemical stimuli), *complete* sensation (the first and the subsequent perception, obtained by the mastication and oxygenation of the food in the mouth, which allows capturing the aromatic and tactile nuances), and *reflective* sensation (the final appreciation and the act of judgment after the ingestion of the food item—a process that can take a long time, if it is true that we are sometimes undecided in evaluating whether we really enjoyed something or not) (Brillat-Savarin 2009). Taste in Calvino's story is a complex system that presupposes these articulations.

Under the Jaguar Sun tells the story of a couple, the writer and his partner Olivia, on vacation in Oaxaca, Mexico, the city of chocolate. Europe's interest in this product, which was initially used as a drink and brought to Spain by the church (Schivelbusch 1992), began here in the sixteenth century. Chocolate, the ambivalent food par excellence, symbol of pleasure and sin, so much so that it appears everywhere in literature and cinema, is not the key player of this story, however. Instead, the story revolves around different foods, seeing taste as a complex device for exploration and as an internal travel compass through Mexico. Here, taste is mostly dressed and related to cultural forces, an adult version of the relationships one bears to oneself and to others. The anthropological trip through food in *Under the Jaguar Sun* leads to reflections and new elaborations on identity and the redefinition of relational strategies. During their travels, the two main characters try many traditional dishes and come to recognize the signs of a highly developed culture: "Olivia remarked that such dishes involved hours and hours of work and, even before that, a long series of experiments and adjustments . . . imagining entire lives devoted to the search for new blends of ingredients, new variations in the measurements, to alert and patient mixing, the handing down of intricate, precise lore" (Calvino 1988, 6). This approach leads to food through an explicit interest in its social and anthropological meanings that precede or follow the act of ingestion and assimilation. The transmission of the art of preparation and the patient alchemy in the transformations, as well as the conflict between the Spanish and the American Indian civilizations and the regional differences in edible material and vocabulary, are all elements that come before or after the perceptual experience. The experience is constituted by an approach *toward* taste, by anticipating it along horizons of expectation and information, the acquisition of historical and anthropological data, and their explicit intellectual elaboration afterward. The trip Olivia and her husband made is a cultural project that lives the experiences of taste as aesthetic experiences. It reflects an attitude toward food that differs highly from naked pleasure as it was discussed in the first chapter. Naked pleasure was, above all, an aesthetic relationship stemming from a "simple" sensory stimulation taken in its relative "narrowness" in an environment. Dressed taste, on the other hand, emphasizes the constructive and *poietic* role of the aesthetic relation. This difference in attitudes does not denote any hierarchy but, pragmatically, different relevant contexts of experience and appropriate narrative processes.

In the following passage, Calvino defines such an aesthetic program with words that are often quoted: "The true journey, as the introjections of an "outside" different from our normal one, implies a complete change of nutrition, a digesting of the visited country— its fauna and flora and its culture (not only the different culinary practices and condiments but the different implements used to grind the flour or stir the pot)—making it pass between the lips and down the esophagus. This is the only kind of travel that has a meaning nowadays, when everything visible you can see on television without rising from your easy chair. (And you mustn't rebut that the same result can be achieved by visiting the exotic restaurants of our big cities; they so counterfeit the reality of the cuisine they claim to follow that, as far as our deriving real knowledge is concerned, they are the equivalent not of an actual locality, but of a scene reconstructed and shot in a studio.)" (1988, 12). Calvino's aesthetic perspective sees in the journey the most radical search for experiential authenticity, and therefore it redefines the hierarchy of the senses as in Nothomb's novels. Instead of a bare perception, however, here we find a semiotics of culture: tasting, the "only kind of travel that has a meaning nowadays," means assimilating "between the lips and down the esophagus," ingesting and physically consuming the object, and this perceptual process can be neither substituted nor replaced, in contrast to what may well happen in visual perception. Taste is the embodied experience that permits the most appropriate knowledge of the other, the perceptual ability that allows a true contact with things, exactly because it does not only touch the matter, but merges with it. Taste establishes a carnal twine between perceiver and perceived. If in the Platonic-Hegelian tradition this mixture expresses the epistemic limit of the so-called minor sense, Calvino instead adopts an alternative paradigm. According to a minority in Western thought, taste guarantees an even higher level of truthfulness: "it informs us in a perfect way concerning the nature of things" because "the entire substance of the tasted object comes into contact with the tongue and penetrates it directly," as an anonymous medieval commentator claimed ("Summa de saporibus" 1991, 231).

Calvino provides a radical meaning to the access to food through dressed taste. In the words of the anthropologist David Le Breton, taste here is the *taste of the world* because it is *knowledge of the world* (Le Breton 2006). It is a knowledge that fuses sharing and bonds, but also lacerations and conflicts. If, with naked pleasure and prereflective enjoyment, sharing, struggles, or guilt feelings occur with respect to infantile behavior or to regression in adulthood, in Calvino's story the context is different. We are faced with a rational conflict between cultivated human beings in whom dressed taste acts as an amplifier or mirror of the discomforts that lie outside the planned management of existence. The perceptual difference between the narrator and his partner surfaces, for instance, in a pragmatics of taste: "Olivia more sensitive to perceptive nuances and endowed with a more analytical memory, where every recollection remained distinct and unmistakable; I tending more to define experiences verbally and conceptually, to mark the ideal line of journey within ourselves contemporaneously with our geographical journey" (Calvino 1988, 11). While Olivia cultivates a gustatory knowledge geared toward intense perceptual attention and tacit memory, the narrator for his part tries to translate the living experience into words and concepts. This difference harks back to the hierarchy between men and women with respect to the kitchen. The domain of taste, of smells, of the body, of practical gestures is a woman's assigned social prerogative; the domain of theory, of conceptualized language, and of ideal design is a man's. Far from being an obsolete prejudice, this still holds true today. Think of the distinction between so-called traditional and creative cuisine, commonly seen as a sharp distinction between the mechanical execution of coded recipes and creative inventive design, and now consider the predominant gender associated with each. There is a French word that expresses this axiology, that is, *chef*. The chef, according to the definition by the French historian Revel, "is a man capable of inventing that which hasn't already been eaten at home" (Baugé 2012). The chef is therefore a *chief*, that is, primarily a head, a mind. The space of the chef is outside of the house, the space of the woman cook is at home. *Women should stay in the kitchen*: this thought expresses the ideology of a precise social structure that involves all aspects of human life (Cooper 1998). The autonomous space of women is carved out within the domestic walls and, above all, expresses itself in cooking and in other tasks that are done in the absence of men, who go out to work, produce, create, and fill public roles. The mouth symbolizes this hierarchical prejudice well, at the same time denoting its ambivalence. It is the opening through which food enters and words exit, a *medium* of the physical and the mental together, and it differently serves sensitive, perceptual, and intellectual needs.

Through taste, Olivia emphasizes haptic and tacit perception; the narrator, on the other hand, emphasizes verbal and conceptual perception, exploring the object and then putting it back at a distance. Olivia lives taste as a harmoniously twofold instrument, "pleasure that knows, knowledge that enjoys," as defined by the Italian philosopher Giorgio Agamben (2015). Knowledge and culture do not weaken but rather enhance pleasure. Instead, for the narrator taste is a problem. He recognizes its potential, but he lives it within a dramatically dualistic frame—tacit, haptic pleasure on the one hand, explicit, theoretical knowledge on the other—whose only solution is a complete translation of taste into conceptual language. Calvino's story therefore provides a good example for dressed taste to be expressed in different manners.

Let's return to the gender issue. The conflict between male and female is repeatedly evoked in Calvino's story, but more generally it can easy be established that, in the Western tradition, the neglect of gustatory perception has always accompanied emotional, erotic, and sexual problems. From the condemnation of physical pleasure and its excess by the more radical versions of the Christian tradition—where gluttony and sex are united by the same interdict—to the opposite glorification of gluttony as a mark of Eros/Thanatos recounted by so much literature and so many films (think of *La grande bouffe*), taste always has a gender connotation, both in physical and in psychic characterizations. Taste as a psychic glue is an interesting variation on the theme for understanding some of the prevailing attitudes in the experience of food: cooking can be a vehicle to seduce, to call back those who are gone, to be forgiven, but it can be also a survival strategy. Olivia and the narrator leave for their trip to Mexico during a marriage crisis, and food is the *medium* chosen for their attempt to reestablish a true sensual relationship. It is not difficult to bring fiction back to real life. At times, the development of the dominance of gustatory experiences in couples is the supplement to, or substitute for, the sensual decline in long-term relationships. This finding is not irrelevant to our theme. We have to know how to frame taste experience in this context with the possibility of an alternative or supplementary performance. This allows us to understand these gustatory attitudes and not condemn them.

DRESSED TASTE, IMAGE, AND REPRESENTATION

In the first chapter, I discussed the fundamental relationship between pleasure and images. The image is the sensory form of every living action, and therefore also of taste perception. A specific triangulation emerged from that mode of access: perceiver and perceived were connected through a medium that intensified, clarified, or let pleasure express itself as "naked." Taste as dressed and codified knowledge has an equally stringent relationship with images, although expressed differently. Just think of the education of taste, of recipe books, or of the endless articulations of the expression "taste is culture" in the mass media (websites, blogs, and television). Gustatory perception is the direct experience of food, therefore a strategy that boosts the aesthetic relationship by drawing on one's embodied capacity and expanding it, but, as with pleasure, the triangulation with images and representations is unavoidable.

In Calvino's story, the relationship between taste perception and visual representation is explicitly advocated. Even though it only points in one direction, thirty years after its first publication, it still contains many useful insights and deserves to be discussed. The savory, aromatic, and haptic experience is seen as a viable and concrete alternative to the static nature of the visual image as it is commonly misunderstood and lived in ordinary experience. Calvino compared the "real" journey to the visited country, as physical ingestion through taste, to the technological and reproducible image-simulacrum of television. However, the issue is not as simple as it seems, and it is the author himself who reminds us of this in another passage of *Under the Jaguar Sun*: "I concentrated on devouring, with every meatball, the whole fragrance of Olivia—through voluptuous mastication, a vampire extraction of vital juices. But I realized that in a relationship that should have been among three terms—me, meatball, Olivia—a fourth term had intruded, assuming a dominant role: the name of the meatballs. It was the name '*gorditas pellizcadas con manteca*' that I was especially savoring and assimilating and possessing" (27). This passage clarifies that the image is not reducible to its bloodless stasis. The bond between taste and language refers here to the acoustic image of the name "*gorditas pellizcadas con manteca*," but its power holds also with respect to visual perception.

In television and cinema, and especially with the explosion of the web over the last decade, we have become witnesses, on the one hand, to a proliferation of food- and taste-related content, conveyed by the visual image, and, on the other, to its progressive virtualization. Food has become a commanding and almost overpowering presence in communication as an expression of the most diverse meanings. And this fact is accompanied by its symmetrical counterpart, the growing interest in visual cuisine and cooks corresponds to the decrease in active cooking. It is as though what Heidegger said about the destiny of modern metaphysics were true for gastronomy too. To paraphrase "The Age of the World Picture" (Heidegger 2002), I would say that today we live in the age of the *Food Picture,* of food reduced to image and simulacrum. Thus, every day we experience the risk—as was already exposed by Roland Barthes (Barthes 1997)—that the gustatory haptic experience in vivo could move to the visual field and be replaced by it. We live in a paradox; while pictures, news, and even food objects proliferate, we are losing our grip on real things, we are losing experiential and life awareness. With respect to taste, this process derived also from what Walter Benjamin named—referring to works of art—reproducibility. According to Benjamin, art has lost its "aura," its uniqueness, its *hic et nunc* (Benjamin 2008) as a result of advanced reproduction technologies. Benjamin's thought developed from a reflection on the "new arts" of that time, photography and film. Similarly, one may argue that the experience of taste has lost the uniqueness of its unrepeatable experience as a result of being reproduced in increasingly sophisticated ways in photos, videos, and movies. However, it is undeniable that there is a fundamental difference between gustatory and (mere) visual perception of taste, due to the material incorporation and assimilation of food. How do things really stand here? The relationship between the experience of eating and its narration through images cannot consist in either a reduction or an adaption of the former to the latter. Instead, we should speak of a translation, even more precisely of an active correspondence between two ontologically different yet intertwined levels. Nothing is more different than eating as compared to watching others eat or contemplate dishes, but since taste is a multisensory perception, sight is a very important influence. That said, it is also undeniable that in everyday life the risk of a virtualization of taste exists and produces different bad practices, such as criticizing and condemning cuisine and chefs using "hearsay" and things "seen," especially online, as well as the power of marketing trends, which produces a trivialized uniformity in judgment and appreciation.

A positive dialogue between taste experience and visual experience does not ignore the necessity of a pictorial dimension of gustatory perception, from naked pleasure to dressed taste. Along these lines, gustatory imagery was compared to theater, as a scene comprising many heterogeneous elements such as muscle movements, gestures, facial expressions, and words. It is very telling that some authors have compared this need with a prosthesis that weakens the importance of taste with respect to sight and hearing, those autonomously symbolic and expressive senses (Leroi-Gourhan 1964–65). But now, on the contrary, also from recent cognitive and psychological research, we can see this as an asset: taste always confronts us with a complex *multisensory* field, so much so that other scholars have even tried to establish correspondences between the gustatory and the visual qualities of a dish.

The representational need of taste can be understood both as a *mental induction* to taste and as its *condition of access*. For instance, a name or a word may produce—or bypass—the taste of food (the name of the meatballs in Calvino's story) because words have to do with the mouth. Words and writing condense taste and image into the imaginary, of course without reducing the real meatball to its sound or its description. Taste perception always signals a surplus of the signifier (food "in itself," while we assimilate it in the concrete relationship) with respect to the signified (its expression and its expressibility). But words and, even more, visual representations have great power. They induce and arouse revulsion and prevent access to certain experiences, as demonstrated by many experiments regarding the conditioning of perception (Taylor 2004; Gueguen 2010). Each verbal or figurative sign refers to a specific horizon of gustatory expectation that activates channels of attention. Chefs are clearly well aware of this, and they sometimes devote much time to the multisensory construction of their dishes, with particular attention not only to appearance, but also to names.

Real gustatory experiences possess a regenerative potential for human existence, having to do with a cultivation of the awareness of one's body and sensitivity. Taste as embodied knowledge can be an effective critical instance for a renewal of deeper experiential modalities. Exploration via dressed taste and the development of specific codes of expression is a thrilling way to access aesthetic experience according to Calvino's *Under the Jaguar Sun*. But, simultaneously, taste can be an ally of the superficial leveling of a vilified feeling devoid of meaning, as the increasing power of media shows us every day. During the same period of Calvino's story, the philosopher Michel Serres issued a warning in his essay "The Five Senses": "The victory of reason: the only taste an apricot has is the taste of the word 'apricot' passing over the lips" (Serres 2008, 233). Taking the approach of taste as knowledge and culture should promote critical and wise attitudes, but that, unfortunately, is not always the case.

TASTE, CONFLICTS, AND CULTURE

Through naked pleasure, the experience of taste molded a perception characterized by ungovernability and passive abandonment. Dressed taste sketches a different way to experience taste, apparently more reasonable and balanced. Culture accompanies and empowers pleasure, returning it to shareability and public language. However, these two approaches are not alternatives. They represent different experiences, different accentuation preferences, which in many cases are even intertwined. In the first mode of access to food, we have shown how, in certain circumstances, naked pleasure touches upon the adult territories of knowledge. Similarly, we must emphasize that, in certain contexts, dressed taste looms close to the borders of impulses not controllable by nature. With a culture's own perceptual devices, some experiences that are directed toward food find themselves hostage to the unexpected powers stemming from areas of our being that are not subject to rational will. In other words, the perception of taste does not have a linear and irreversible evolution; it is distinguished, instead, by reversibility and circularity, which can take different characterizations. For example, the philosopher Jacques Derrida, in certain analyses based on the *Critique of the*

Power of Judgment by Kant, identified *vomit* as the limit of digestion, the extreme expression of external matter that cannot be assimilated by our psychophysical system (and that is not necessarily disgusting: we often vomit what we ate with great pleasure) (Derrida, 1981).

In *Under the Jaguar Sun*, the blind spot and the limit of resistance to the domain of gustatory reason are presented under the disturbing guise of anthropophagy and cannibalism, which Olivia introduces during a discussion of sacrificial cuisine with their local guide. The taste for human flesh explicitly emerges at the end of the story; it goes beyond the field of cultural anthropology and establishes itself as the telos of the gustatory experience, taking on a metaphorical and universal meaning: "Under the thatched arbor of a restaurant on a riverbank, where Olivia had waited for me, our teeth began to move slowly, with equal rhythm, and our eyes stared into each other's with the intensity of serpents'—serpents concentrated in the ecstasy of swallowing each other in turn, as we were aware, in our turn, of being swallowed by the serpent that digests us all, assimilated cease-lessly in the process of ingestion and digestion, in the universal can-nibalism that leaves its imprint on every amorous relationship and erases the lines between our bodies and *sopa de frijoles, huacinango a la veracruzana,* and *enchiladas*" (Calvino 1988, 29). As some scholars point out, following a Hegelian perspective, "universal cannibalism" corre-sponds to a similar structure of understanding. Understanding (the other) is assimilating, ingesting, and metabolizing (the Latin *com-prehendo* refers to the act of grasping, of taking something with your hands and holding it). Here, the vital metabolic process turns into a metaphor of the human as such, to the extent that living means being in society, and every social relationship is a process of recogni-tion of the other, but also at the same time of his or her assimilation. Again, what is here at play is not unrelated to the question of gender. Take the sexual act, for example: the man, unlike the woman, makes love by possessing and being taken in (Derrida 1992). Literature also features many examples of disgust and repulsion—a notion and experience in which philosophers are perhaps much more interested than in taste. To take a famous example, in chapter 64 of Melville's *Moby Dick*, the second mate Stubb shares his dinner of whale-steak freshly cut from the animal just caught with a plethora of sharks that finish off the carcass in the water. The description of the scene conveys a sense of horror and disgust, but it is also a reflection on the life cycle and on the relationship between eating and being eaten (Korsmeyer 1999).

In Calvino's poetics, the gustatory experience often plays an exemplary and metaphorical role. From *Mr. Palomar* to *Cosmicomics*, food and flavors appear regarding questions of Eros, of the role of the human being in the universe, and of social and historical relationships. In one of his most famous novels, *The Baron in the Trees*, the story of Cosimo, who decided to live in trees, follows from an act of rejection of some food due to its taste. Cosimo's protest becomes totally political. The narrator, Cosimo's brother, describes the family atmosphere by way of the family meals. The tension between the father and children, in particular Battista, Cosimo's sister, emerges here: "So it can be seen why our family board brought out all the antagonisms, the incompatibilities, between us, and all our follies and hypocrisies too; and why it was there that Cosimo's rebellion came to a head" (Calvino 1977, 6). Cosimo rebels against his sister because he is disgusted by the strange dishes she prepares—*crostini* of rat liver pate, grasshopper legs, roasted pig tails, "horrible dishes"—and, in particular, by snails. The conflict turns into a war of taste involving identity-related paths and experiences, a whole framework of relations that cannot be reduced to the pure, naked pleasure of the palate but rather refers back to the family meal, to the meal as a communal and conflicting moment. The anthropology of food has given much thought to the relationship between "good to eat" and "good to think": Lévi-Strauss's famous thesis argued that what communities like to eat is what is (considered as) good to think in a moral sense. In Lévi-Strauss's paradigm, food aesthetics follows from food ethics. This was overturned by Marvin Harris in a more materialistic sense. What communities find ethically good in food habits is what they *must* eat for geographic, economic, and historical reasons. According to the general movement of this essay, again it is not necessary to choose between one of the two options. Gustatory taste grows in the intertwining of ethics and aesthetics, and it operates each time on different levels according to the environmental experience. The gustatory multisensory perceptual system contains ethical and economic instances, as well as physiological and aesthetic ones. As we have shown, taste is an *ecological* perception: it consists of an amalgam of heterogeneous forces—from chemical stimuli to highest cognitive levels—that at times also express conflicting values. This is why taste experiences are many and varied, and for this reason, we sometimes taste with a passive, abandoned attitude, sometimes by way of firmly established cultural codes and patterns, and most of the time playing on both accesses according to different scales and intensities. In the ecological and pragmatic perspective of the aesthetic relationship, one must understand that the perceptual approaches to taste are different and respond to different criteria of distinction, different desires, different projects and goals.

Under the Jaguar Sun crosses the territory of taste on hot and spicy flavors. That is to say, adult flavors, the bitterness of cocoa and coffee, the spiciness of chili. The intellectual appreciation of taste usually comes into play when the food involved is difficult (think of "high cuisine" dishes), strange, or exotic. Exoticism concerns our discussion, because it is the approach to the other that is in question, the interplay with different styles and cultures, as well as with different stages in one's life: wine, tea, coffee, and high cuisine express the adult appreciation for mediated taste. These foods are social markers; they mark the entry into certain groups. Think of the first glass of red wine, with its acidity and tannins, and how the process of appreciation develops here. The fact that training and education are involved in this category of foods seems intuitive. Why should we have to learn the taste of childhood on which we built our first relationships with others? This would seem useless and bizarre, but this is not always so. On the one hand, owing to different circumstances, some people are estranged from their own childhood tastes, and it is also due to this fact that in postindustrial Western societies a new educational question regarding taste is thriving, which is not geared toward the exotic, but rather toward the local and the familiar and goes by the name of "tradition." From time to time, celebrity chefs create "childish" dishes, which explicitly evoke gustatory dimensions "surpassed" in individual growth. On the other hand, globalization has changed the dynamic between the exotic and the local. It can happen that the foreign becomes more familiar than the formerly familiar ones, and that the boundaries of the known and the unknown are modified. These remarks show that relying on the notion of "culture" in general is not enough, when taste experiences are at play. A specific perspective and an appropriate narrative are needed to understand time and again what kind of relationship is involved between the perceiver, the food perceived, and the environment. Taste is a multimodal device, embedded, relational, flexible, and *potentially* skilled at sorting out very different and even opposite situations.

CURIOSITY, EXPERTISE, CRITICISM (WITH RISKS INCLUDED)

Walter Benjamin believed architecture to be an emblematic case of an art that has a collective and routine use. The appropriate experience of architecture—precisely because it responds to practical uses and because its original function is not visual contemplation but rather dwelling interaction—amounts to a perception that he defined as "distracted." The question posed by Benjamin was part of a major aesthetic debate regarding the nature of a work of art. In the wake of Benjamin, we can address in our context the following similar question. Do food experts and critics, with their analytical dissections of gustatory processes, incarnate the most appropriate way to live taste perception? From an evolutionary point of view, the first and primary function of food has been to feed and to feed well. In parallel, the first and primary function of taste has been to escape harmful and toxic foods, and then to make us feel good and give us pleasure. An aesthetics of taste should start then from this fact: all edible matter, even the most refined, is picked, bred, or made to be eaten. And all food, even that of the most refined gastronomic quality, retains its nutritional and energy-providing function. Why then should we assume that the cultivation of gustatory perception aimed at appreciating taste stems from the removal of this very basic but essential fact in favor of a mere analysis of flavor? I believe this approach depends on the preponderance of the visual and contemplative paradigm of aesthetics, according to which the true appreciation of food and drink must pass through an analytical exploration made by our sensory/perceptual apparatus. The haptic process of tasting is then considered as if it were observed by an eye. However, this approach surreptitiously presupposes what it sets out to prove, namely, that to appreciate food requires analyzing it in discrete terms, dissecting the object of appreciation into separate moments like the color, the odor, the taste. I do not reject the legitimacy of food being appreciated *also* in reflective and analytical ways, as I suggest that taste perception is molded in many different environmental experiences that take many different forms. I am merely asserting that this is not the *only* possible approach or the only way to appreciate it. We can appreciate food *aesthetically* also taking a different way, just considering its physical and psychological effects and its transformation into energy for life. This implies accepting a different conception of aesthetics, based on material contact, assimilation, and metabolism. To wholly understand the aesthetics of taste, it is necessary to go beyond the privilege of vision and the formal perspective that supports it. We should value instead the vital and metabolic aspects, as well as transformation and change, because taste always leaves a trace, even if you cannot see it.

Adult, thoughtful, and cultural gustative appreciation passes through different stages. Historical and anthropological curiosity is usually the first stage. Bertrand Russell was not particularly interested in food, but he was a curious and certainly very intelligent person. He once made a very interesting observation: "I have enjoyed peaches and apricots more since I have known that they were first cultivated in China in the early days of Han Dynasty; that Chinese hostages held by the great King Kaniska introduced them to India, whence they spread to Persia, reaching the Roman Empire in the first century of our era; that the word "apricot" is derived from the same Latin source as the word "precocious," because the apricot ripens early; and that the A at the beginning was added by mistake, owing to a false etymology. All this makes the fruit taste much sweeter" (2004, 25). The passage clearly shows that taste can be directly stimulated by cultural factors such as historical knowledge and extrasensory elements, which may affect the moment of perception itself. The degree of conditioning varies with the tasting subject. It is no coincidence that a "simple" curious person can point out the link between information received and perceived gustative pleasure ("much sweeter"). Just prior to the quoted passage, Russell writes that "curious learning not only makes unpleasant things less unpleasant, but also makes pleasant things more pleasant." Extrasensory information that does not refer to the intrinsic characteristics of the foodstuff and that is intended rather to arouse interest and attraction, creating a sort of "aura" of uniqueness around the object, is what many marketing strategies and also many contextualized everyday experiences offer.

If one evening, in a fit of generosity, I were to offer a special bottle of wine to some friends who are everything but "foodies," I would not offer it "blindly" without saying a word (unless I wanted to perform another experiment about the universal and absolute perception of good). But neither would I describe its particular aesthetic and nonaesthetic gustative properties, for they would not understand them, lacking the vocabulary provided by expertise. I could tell them something about the wine's historical and cultural importance, its myth, and also its market price. In this way, I would capture their attention and create a horizon of expectation and perceptive curiosity that could lead to their drinking with appreciative awareness and not in a mechanical and ignorant fashion. This would not be enough to create awareness, but it would be a suggestion, a signal for a path to be walked. Were I to offer the same wine to connoisseurs, I would not say those things because they could be taken for granted. More importantly, because of the nascent established relationship between the guests, the wine, and myself, it will develop further from gustatory perception as such, and then possibly turn to extrasensory data ex post. Here, too, I am not describing a straightforward and imposed process. Not all curious people become experts and not all experts become experts by following the same training and process.

There are wine experts who have acquired their experience exclusively via sensory training, without any historical, anthropological, or geographical knowledge. Do they enjoy less? It depends on the occasions. In order to enjoy and appreciate food, knowledge as the voluntary *accumulation* of information and culture is not *always* necessary, but relational aesthetic sensitivity is. Of course, culture *can* help in developing a more accurate and critical perception, but again this is not always the case since cultural organization can also be subject to the same standardizations as production processes. In this light, criticism is important, but at the same time, we should not forget that the main purpose of food—to nourish well and to arouse pleasure—suggests taking the issue of criticism lightly.

The highest social mark of distinction for the cultivation of taste is expertise. The food expert is someone skilled in some particular product, like wine or beer, or in the gastronomic experience in general such as fine dining. Wine experts are traditionally more common in Western society, but there are also experts in spirits, cheese, cured meat, and chocolate. In Eastern society, tea ceremony expertise is very well known. Being an expert regarding products is different from being an expert on taste in general terms. The latter case presupposes a developed sensitivity, not solely geared to the object but to many different features: styles, traditions, contextual goals. In other words, being a gastronome does not mean being an expert on every single ingredient tasted; it means being experienced in how the final combination, the dishes, their sequence, the whole menu, and the overall experience, comes to be. A restaurant serving traditional Tuscan fare, for example, will have certain standards of reference, with respect to the ingredients, the recipes, their elaboration, and maybe even the atmosphere. The expert should be able to interpret and evaluate these factors along with many others, offering consistent and reasonable grounds for her assessments. The learning process of a gastronome is an interesting experience because, unlike what one might think, it does not involve only the sensory training during food intake.

Undoubtedly, it is necessary to train one's senses in order to perceive what nonexperts do not perceive. As David Hume already asserted in the middle of the eighteenth century in his well-known essay "Of the Standard of Taste": "A good palate is not tried by strong flavors, but by a mixture of small ingredients, where we are still sensible of each part, notwithstanding its minuteness and its confusion with the rest" (Hume 1909–14, §17). However, the attention needed for good gustative perception is only part of the path that leads to expertise. One must focus on the surroundings of taste, what precedes it, what constitutes it, and what follows. John Dewey stated this well: "Even the pleasures of the palate are different in quality to an epicure than in one who merely 'likes' his food as he eats it. The different is not of mere intensity. The epicure is conscious of much more than the taste of the food. Rather there enter into the taste, as directly experienced, qualities that depend upon reference to its source and its manner of production in connection with criteria of excellence. As production must absorb into itself qualities of the product as perceived and be regulated by them, so, on the other side, seeing, hearing, tasting, become esthetic when relation to a distinct manner of activity qualifies what is perceived" (1980, 50–51). In this mode of experience, taste should function as an antenna designed to capture meanings and values of different orders: aesthetic, ethical, economic, political, and social. The taste expert, both the enthusiast/connoisseur and the professional critic, should therefore be an example of equilibrium, openness, vision, and sensitivity, as suggested again by Hume: "Strong sense, united to delicate sentiment, improved by practice, perfected by comparison, and cleared of all prejudice, can alone entitle critics to this valuable character; and the joint verdict of such, wherever they are to be found, is the true standard of taste and beauty" (1909–14, §23).

Often, however, reality shows us a very different approach to expertise. An extreme characterization of the risk of compulsiveness that leads to a dramatic disease is depicted in Paul Torday's novel *The Irresistible Inheritance of Wilberforce*, in which the main character, Wilberforce, develops a slowly increasing curiosity about wine driven by conscious existential unhappiness, a successful but unrewarding career, and almost no affective relationships. The passion for wine grants him access to a new, emotionally active, and fascinating social life. Wilberforce now begins to invest the time he had so far spent anonymously on his career affectively and emotionally, but along the way he falls prey to his love. Wine becomes an all-encompassing investment and, through the lens of a more refined expertise, a compulsive obsession. He becomes fanatical about great Bordeaux wines and consumes more and more until he turns into an alcoholic. The story of Wilberforce is the story of a man who discovers unprecedented experiences that shed unexpected meaning on new passions by living the taste experience as knowledge and as pleasure to its fullest. However, he loses the balance necessary for their "positive" incorporation and dies. In a very significant point of the novel, the weak boundaries of pleasure, knowledge, and pathology within one and the same experience become clear. Wilberforce has tried tackling his addiction in a center for alcohol abuse. Upon returning home, he reflects, "Meanwhile, it had been a very long time since I had drunk a glass of wine. With, I admit, trembling hands, I found the last bottle of Chateau Carbonnieux and opened it. An alcoholic, *which I am not and never have been*, would not have sat and let it breathe for half an hour, and let it come up towards room temperature. He would not have poured it lovingly into the large bowl of a tasting glass, to ensure the bouquet could develop properly. Nor would he have checked the glass first for any mustiness. . . . An alcoholic would not have rolled the purple liquid gently around in the glass, to capture the aroma of the wine, and then taken a single sip, allowing the complex chemicals of the wine to release themselves upon his tongue. He would not have made the effort to *characterize the tastes from the wine* in the approved wine taster's vocabulary: sweet black cherries, toasty oak in the background" (Torday 2008, 71–72, my emphasis). Wilberforce excuses his addiction, denying both its seriousness and its real name, "alcoholism," by referring to the cultural dominance of the field and his absolute expertise. An analogous defensive strategy is found frequently in real life among gastronomes, both enthusiasts and experts, though in less serious cases than those of poor Wilberforce. It is as though the "drawbacks of the trade" were enough to ennoble a practice, to redeem it from the "lowliness" of instincts and toxins.

There are other, less explicit, and more subtle types of addiction and compulsive behavior. Some experts and critics are victims of a true obsessive-compulsive disorder regarding the food they should be appreciating and evaluating in a levelheaded fashion. If classic iconography portrays the fat gastronome in the act of smelling or tasting, his nose deep in a glass of wine or close to a piece of meat or cheese, today we can witness new forms of foodism modeled on different tools—computers, digital cameras, smartphones—that sometimes complement and enhance the body's perceptual apparatus according to a consistent evolutionary process, and at other times tend to replace it instead. Recording data and archiving images in some cases appear to stand for the living perceptual experience, as if what really mattered were documenting the fact that "I've had that experience" rather than enjoying and critically reflecting on the experience itself. Just as naked pleasure risks becoming autistic and infantile if it does not develop and evolve, surviving in the appropriate contextual circumstances, dressed taste can degenerate into a narcissistic discourse in spite of any true relational perception. An expert may lose the value of the intellectual pleasure of tasting (this is the sense of appreciation through knowledge) because he focuses on the *analytical* observation of food and its components. Wittgenstein once expressed this aesthetic misunderstanding, arguing that anybody who read the description of a monument or sculpture instead of *looking* at it would lack the perceptual experience of why that object was created. The object is read regardless of its interaction with the perceiver; the perceiver acts as a neutral medium of presumed pure knowledge. This may lead to a recognition of taste, as it were, made of already known elements, as it was handed over to codes that are already known and assimilated, eliminating any possible new cognition and any surprise effect. In this situation, one perceives in a dulled fashion, hurriedly and distractedly, and maybe even accepts the fashion of the moment. If, in the experience of naked pleasure, the risk was canceling any real otherness as well as the very self that constitutes itself through it by way of an enjoyment that unilaterally abandoned itself to the object, the risk of dressed taste is instead an "epistemological abuse," a cognitive obsession where the otherness of the matter paradoxically almost disappears.

In some cases, the degeneration described above becomes an exercise in power, both in professional criticism and in everyday taste experiences, when the gastronome flaunts his haughty ways in his small playground. A few years ago, this figure was masterfully described by the authors of *Ratatouille*, the well-known Disney movie starring the rat chef Remy. One of the main characters of the story is the much-feared food critic Anton Ego. In a famous scene, he critically reflects on his work: "In many ways, the work of a critic is easy. We risk very little, yet enjoy a position over those who offer up their work and their selves to our judgment. We thrive on negative criticism, which is fun to write and to read. But the bitter truth we critics must face is that, in the grand scheme of things, the average piece of junk is more meaningful than our criticism designating it so. But there are times when a critic truly risks something, and that is in the discovery and defense of the new." This remark provides many suggestions. Anton Ego is consumed by his ego: narcissism and loneliness lead to compulsive, excessive, and pedantic behavior. This compulsion is expressed in different ways. It may concern the boundless need for information on the genealogy of food, *orthorexia* (the excessive preoccupation with avoiding food perceived to be unhealthy), or the paroxysm of analytical recognition of the elements that make up a dish or a wine—ingredients, cooking methods, spices, flavors, or textures. Again, I am not denying the importance of higher sensory skills, developed through specific and long training. On some occasions, it is important to grasp all the elements to complete an assessment and enrich appreciation. But qualitative assessment normally passes through a total *synthetic* appreciation, and only afterward can it be broken down into discrete data, for an ex post understanding of the appreciated item and experience. A comparison with music may be helpful here: the appreciation of a piece of music lies in listening, not in reading the score. Of course, this can be most useful for certain purposes, but it should not trump the open act of listening. In this light, at the end of the film, Anton Ego repents and embraces a more open and "amateur" perspective on taste perception, one that can also be supported by convincing philosophical, psychological, and sociological arguments. The same position can also be found in another literary food critic, Monsieur Arthens, one of the main characters of Muriel Barbery's *Gourmet Rhapsody* whom we have already met in the first chapter. At the end of his life, Arthens, by now bedridden, asks his grandson to grant him one culinary wish: some cream puffs. Not the best ones in town, but the supermarket cream puffs he loved to eat on his way to school. The great and refined critic's last perception is reconciled with the pure and vulgar pleasure of the beginning: "In the almost mystical union between my tongue and these supermarket chouquettes, with their industrial batter and their treacly sugar, I attained God. Since then, I have lost him, sacrificed him to the glorious desires which were not mine" (Barbery 2000, 155). The attitudes of Ego at the end of *Ratatouille* and of Arthens on his deathbed well express that flexible and multimodular perception that taste permits when properly heard and cultivated.

The basic function of food does not conflict with the cultivation of taste, if by "cultivating taste" we do not only reductively mean a social mark of distinction and hierarchy, but instead a tool of social understanding, self-care, and listening to others. Beyond gastronomy, one of the general and classic problems of criticism concerns the connection between expert judgment and public acceptance of it, the connection between the critic's seemingly designated task—promoting and communicating "good" taste on the basis of "standard" and valuable parameters—and what the public actually likes, something that tastes "good." A few years ago, an American advertising campaign for a brand of canned tuna summarized this conflict very effectively: "Star-Kist doesn't want tunas with good taste. They want tunas that taste good" (Iggers 2007, 95). This highlights the reversal of the hierarchy of values in mass society; what really matters is what most people like, not what a few claim to be better. The gap between expertise and ignorance has been increasingly hidden and maybe even erased today, when every cultural, aesthetic, and artistic expression, from the most highbrow and exclusive events to the most ordinary and vulgar ones, can attain "pop" fruition thanks to the enhancing powers of technological devices. Gastronomy is one of the most evident examples of such phenomenon in contemporary society, so much so that many people wonder if the figure of the iconic food critic personified by Anton Ego and Monsieur Arthens still plays a decisive role. In fact, pop food culture is highly involved in the discussion about digital democracy. On the web, many attempts at "grassroots" criticism canceling any representation or authority of good taste are made with sites and servers collecting feedback on products and services and then compiling charts and statistics. However, this trend reveals another facet of the prejudice according to which quality is quantity and numbers that correspond to the sum of all individual preferences. Disregarding the mediation of authority, dressed taste loses the characteristics of a socially constituted and negotiated value among those who became experts through training and learning, and instead becomes a battleground for blind, anonymous, and purely numerical forces. According to our proposal of taste as a flexible experience, the two instances—effectively educated, sanctioned expertise and criticism on one side, and the vulgarization of taste judgments and values on the other—are not mutually exclusive; rather, they need to interact and intertwine. One would have to be blind not to observe that food critics today cannot take Anton Ego as their example. At the same time, it would also be very superficial to take the lawless processes of the democratization and popularization of taste as the arrival points of a democratic and self-generating transparency. The processes leading to the assignment of values are never neutral and objective in the naive sense of the term, since the notion of emotional and aesthetic "value" is an inherently social notion (Shapin 2012).

Taste and Sustainability: The Good That Grounds the Good

A remarkable approach to taste as culture is the ethical appreciation of taste. So far we have seen ethics "percolate" from the uniqueness of the gustatory experience. This approach reverses the perspective where evaluation and judgment grow and develop *before* perceptual encounter. There are many clear examples such as religious dietary laws, whose regimens govern abstinence or moderation according to their purity or to the calendar. However, there are also many, at least apparently, nonreligious ethics that subscribe to the idea that aesthetics is anchored in ethics. Duty lays the foundations for pleasure, such as in vegetarians and vegan models, fair trade, associations that promote food culture, and, more generally, critical gastronomy based on the idea of environmental sustainability (Petrini 2007; Pollan 2006, 2008). A political conviction and an epistemic conviction are the foundation for the ethical appreciation of taste. The latter evaluates aesthetic pleasure and appreciation as secondary or, in its more radical versions, subordinate to the sense of duty as "acting rightly" on the basis of a subscription to the idea—whether informed or not, it hardly matters—that ethics is the first philosophy. This approach sees food as a powerful tool for political change, so good taste must correspond to *fair* (Lemke 2008)

One of the best examples of the ethical appreciation of taste is proposed by the American essayist Wendell Berry. In an essay titled "The Pleasures of Eating," he writes, "The pleasure of eating should be an extensive pleasure, not that of the mere gourmet. . . . I mentioned earlier the politics, esthetics, and ethics of food. But to speak of the pleasure of eating is to go beyond those categories. Eating with the fullest pleasure—pleasure, that is, that does not depend on ignorance—is perhaps the profoundest enactment of our connection with the world" (Berry 1990, 151–52). This is an explicit manifesto: pleasure refers to a broader sentiment, governed by knowledge and ethical reasoning. Gustatory appreciation for food requires a primary sensitivity that can be found in the deeper understanding of our "connection with the world" and that allows the "pleasure of eating" to become "an extensive pleasure" that is not reducible to palatal appreciation while ingesting food. According to this model, education and taste training are primarily oriented not toward gustatory perception but toward an overall educational project that one might define as "sustainable sensoriality" or the desire to direct perceptive values toward an ethical appropriateness. In other words, to have good taste, one must have good rational beliefs. One must understand that taste is formed through conditioning and interests, as a result of which we risk being manipulated and food is likely to be considered a mere commodity. It is a matter not only of contextualizing perceptual experience, but of overloading taste with elements that seem distant and unrelated to gastronomy "in the strict sense." Gastronomy thus changes its traditional characteristics; it both shrinks (less importance is given to taste perception and expertise itself) and grows as an atmospheric mark almost without limits, becoming the expression of a general modus vivendi. This approach is not entirely new; in fact, it goes as far back as the vegetarian regimens of Greek philosophers such as Pythagoras and Plutarch, to the choice of organic or biodynamic production methods, and to certain trends in contemporary culinary research that are increasingly carving out the link between creation and ethical responsibility. Let's take vegetarianism as an example. The choice to not eat meat may stem from animal-rights ethics (animal suffering), from environmental ethics (the energy-related and ecological costs of factory farming), from a religious precept, or from questions of health. In all these cases, taste aligns itself with a prior conviction, with a preliminary orientation.

We could, however, ask in what sense preliminary ethical choices really translate into the gustatory appreciation of food. In other words, does ethically and morally "good" food *always* taste better (Perullo 2014)? And will this ethical approach be able to orient the grammar of taste definitively? I believe there is no simple answer. Ethical appreciation of food is an interesting and complex attitude, but it is not without problems. First, it may risk forgetting the chronological priority in the evolutionary development of our relationship with food. We are not born adults and childhood is a crucial time in our lives. Strictly separating ethics and aesthetics, as some references sometimes seem to suggest, seems to promote an accidental paradox; sometimes sustainable taste becomes the updated version of modern day "good taste," a correct and comfortable trend, widely followed for purely fashion reasons. Consider, for example, the risk of a degeneration that affects the notions of "natural" and "organic," ever more subject to violent semantic and commercial fraud as sedatives for commercial ends used to gain consumer trust and confidence. I am keen on organic and biodynamic food and wine; I find them interesting and often fulfilling. The problem is that sometimes they are an alibi for not increasing one's perceptual awareness and mindful ability to practice environmental tasting. There is also a further problem. The main psychological factor in consumer food choice is pleasure, not ethics (Glanz et al. 1998). Therefore, an optimizing strategy that disregards food's impulsive and hedonic dimension might turn out not to be very effective. Better to pursue a more versatile and lay gustatory model that can hold together the hedonic and the ethical motive, gustative desirability and its moral appropriateness. And moreover, in everyday life don't we often see the very advocates of regulative food ethics let themselves go and indulge in naked pleasure, in their own idiosyncrasies and biographies, suspending and putting aside ethical beliefs and cultural motivations even if only for the moment?

TASTE AND DIET

A variant of ethical appreciation deserves to be very briefly considered. It is a vast, almost pervasive topic, but here I want to suggest only a connection with our theme. There is one way to approach taste as culture primarily or exclusively oriented to the nutritional and dietary aspects of food. For very long time, food, taste, and diet were very strictly bound together; with modern times, they drifted apart. Today's meaning of diet is different and much more limited than the original. Etymologically the word *diet*—from the ancient Greek *diaíta*—meant way of life, matters related to daily activities such as physical exercise, sleep, sexual activity and, of course, alimentation. Food played a great role in diet, so much so that "dietetics" then came to indicate that branch of medicine that deals with food. It was based on the principles of *Hippocratic-Galenic* medicine, grounded in the four elements (earth, water, air, and fire) corresponding to as many qualities (dry, wet, cold, and hot), humors (black bile, yellow bile, phlegm, and blood), and temperaments or characters (melancholic, choleric, phlegmatic, and sanguine). Ancient and medieval dietetics claim that every food has at least one corresponding quality. Eating well means measuring and mixing the various food qualities in order to obtain an equilibrium of moods and temperaments (Flandrin and Montanari 1999). The taste for food corresponded in large part to this interpretative model of reality, and historical documents attest to the close link between taste as pleasure and as health. Taste was in fact mainly the result of dietary reasoning, and it was only in the early modern period that the "liberation of the gourmet," as the French historian Jean-Louis Flandrin called it, was born with a new paradigm of taste based on the palatal perception of single elements of food, regardless of its effects on the body and mind. In the nineteenth century, gastronomy by and large freed itself from dietetics as health, but in the meantime, dietetics has taken on completely different characteristics, because medical science has changed since Hippocrates and Galen. If back then the main proof of the link between taste and diet was based on the *perception* of foodstuffs, because the elements of reality and the qualities—wet, cold, dry, hot—were perceivable qualities, modern science is instead grounded in (trust in the existence of) components of invisible reality: atoms, electrons, cells, and molecules, which are not detectable by the human eye. The same can be said of vitamins, amino acids, minerals, and the lipids and proteins that make up food, but it is exactly on these components that modern nutritional science, as well as the specific branch of dietetics, relies.

In recent years, however, that modern dualistic paradigm has failed once again. Many chefs work with great consideration for *healthiness*, *lightness*, and *balance* in terms of nutrients (calorie count) and food quality (freshness, seasonality) that make up their dishes and menus. Yet regarding the most common experiences with food, the attention to the link between nutrition and taste exploded: food literature contains a virtually limitless number of titles on diets. On the one hand, of course they guarantee important sales figures, but on the other side today the word *diet* encompasses all that goes under the name of *wellness*. In this perspective, eating well and eating the good mean *healthy* eating. It could also be argued that *diet* sometimes becomes a stand-in for faith and other apodictic postulates: health is truth, a recipe for prêt-a-porter happiness, though the common approach of accepting as "healthy" everything that is offered by nutritional science can itself be called into question (Shapin 2007). The connection between food and health is envisaged in different ways with varying intensity, which one must be able to distinguish, ranging from an attitude of simple "common sense" in accordance with popularized scientific knowledge to compulsive and obsessive attitudes such as orthorexia. The formula of the popular "Mediterranean diet" is well known (for example, eat carbohydrates for lunch and protein in the evening, plenty of fruit and vegetables, and few sweets and drink little alcohol). Less common is the habit of alternating between gluttony and health (alternating periods of disregard for nutritional balance and weight control, and very strict periods of almost complete abstinence from "dangerous" foods), and there is also the belief that a food is only good *because* it does good. Of course, there is also an approach to food that redirects all attention to its nutrients, with an utter indifference to its taste. But this attitude goes beyond the scope of this chapter and will be treated in the next.

Third Mode of Access

Indifference

Since in eating pleasure and necessity go together, we fail to discern
between the call of necessity and the seduction of pleasure.
—GREGORY THE GREAT

And now, a dramatic turn of events: the third mode of access to gustatory experience appears to be its negation. After pleasure and knowledge, we have to face indifference toward taste. In the architectonics of food aesthetics, this connects to our thesis: the mindful comprehension of eating experiences comes by way of understanding their entire ranges and processes. Tasting is an activity that is a counterpoint to other oral activities such as breathing, talking, and even eating without tasting. In other words, our experience does not consist of a texture comprising seamless gustatory acts. Taste experiences alternate with other, even more frequent non-taste-related ones, according to a rhythm that is discrete, not continuous, *even* when they involve ingesting food. However, in the ecological and systemic perspective advocated here, these different experiences are related to one another and often intertwined.

By "indifference toward taste" I mean neither disgust nor abstention from food. In this chapter, the indifference will have nothing to do with ascetic aversions to food, or with the huge problem of eating disorders codified by medicine and psychology. Gustatory indifference is not the indifference to food so masterfully described by Kafka in "A Hunger Artist." Here the main character practices the "art of fasting," staging performances of hunger until the surprise ending, in which the hunger artist says that the real reason for his fasting is that he never found food he liked. Gustatory indifference is simply the experience of eating without any attention to the tastes of food or to the act of tasting itself. This is a mainly privative attitude, a nutritional passivity due to a lack of care and perceptive attention toward what is being ingested. It was this attitude we came across in Amélie Nothomb's *The Character of Rain*, where Amélie kept eating the same food with complete indifference for the first two years of her life while feeling like a passive tube.

Looking carefully at this kind of carelessness, one can discover interesting facts and create new connections that allow overcoming old prejudices with respect to eating. The first prejudice calls upon Brillat-Savarin: according to his conception of gastronomy—which has become the most influential one—eating with indifference would seem to be characteristic of a certain animal attitude. For the author of *The Physiology of Taste*, "Animals feed themselves; men eat; but only wise men know the art of eating" (Brillat-Savarin 2009, 15) and "the real enjoyment of eating is a special prerogative of man" (54). The "supremacy of man" establishes an anthropocentric doctrine of taste. And the French gastronome goes on, "[Man], king of all nature by divine right, and for whose benefit the earth has been covered and peopled, must perforce be armed with an organ which can put him in contact with all that is toothsome among his subjects. The tongue of an animal is comparable in its sensitivity to his intelligence. . . . Man's tongue, on the other hand, by the delicacy of its surfaces and of the various membranes which surround it, proves clearly enough the sublimity of the operations for which it is destined" (54–55). In Western philosophy the difference between man and animal is characterized by various oppositions, for example, that between response and reaction (human language elaborates responses to external stimuli, animal vocalizations are only reactions). Within this strong and axiological hierarchy, we can also play the opposition between human taste as a social and cultural mark and mere animal nutrition. But the anthropocentric view about taste makes incorrect scientific assumptions and leads to philosophically incorrect theses. Today ethological and zoosemiotic research tends to prove the existence of animal taste preferences for some species (Martinelli 2010). Building upon Darwin, evolutionary aesthetics takes into account the existence of basic protoaesthetics, which includes not only the primary ability of being able to choose an appropriate object but also that of enjoying it.

The anthropocentrism of taste marks an erroneous ideology of gastronomy as *good* taste, which would radically distance itself from its nutritional bases, an exclusivist hierarchy that is not adequately supported. An aesthetics of taste that also pays attention to the experience of indifference adopts an oblique strategy to combat and overcome these hypostatized dichotomies. Taking care of our nutritional needs does not mean limiting these to the animal basic level. It is instead the first and necessary step to correspond to the original aesthetic input, even when it is not consciously fulfilled. If taste is not of interest, the eating experience happens differently. The food eaten is met differently than a "tasted object" is. Addressing indifference thus helps us cultivate awareness of a more open gastronomy, a gastronomy that is willing to accept differences in taste as outcomes of ecological variations rather than as radical oppositions.

Essen Non Est Percipi

Indifference to taste can take on different meanings and result in different attitudes. As we will see below, there is chronic indifference but there is also circumstantial and appropriate indifference—one could even call it "necessary"—to the unfolding of experience, so as to make it an *aesthetically* legitimate modality. I already stated that there is a very close relationship between indifference and nutrition in the fabric of everyday life. Before tackling the meaning of indifference to taste, then, I need to propose a few more specific considerations regarding the concept of nutrition.

We should first highlight that nutrition is not nutritionism. The latter corresponds to the paradigm according to which the individual nutrients in a food determine its overall nutritional value and (to many) its value in general. The underlying idea is that the whole is equal to the sum of its parts; to know the real essence of food, this position assumes, one should start from its single components. Instead, the position that I defend takes nourishment itself as a *value*, restoring it to its rightful horizon of complexity and beauty, and not reducing it to a mere sum of nutritious ingredients. And yet, this almost trivial truth about the value of nourishment is often masked by the assumption that it is necessary to "dress" taste with the outfit of culture in order to give dignity to the alimentary act. To argue that humans do not only eat and that food is not only nourishment is certainly a truism, but it is equally a truism to remind ourselves that humans *must* eat and that food is, first of all, nourishment. The only way to escape banality is to explore deeply the intrinsic philosophical value of nutrition and feeding. Emanuel Lévinas—highly influenced by Jewish thought, in which the importance and the enjoyment of food are fully legitimated, and in general play a more important role than in the Christian tradition—was the only philosopher of the twentieth century to have conceived nourishment as an essential structure of intentionality. According to Lévinas, the most appropriate image of the intentional structure of experience is someone eating bread. We have already mentioned the passage in which he states that we do not eat to live, but rather eat because we are hungry, and now we can connect it to our new acquisitions. This statement emphasizes how the primary nutritional expression corresponds to a *conatus*, a vital impulse that is not "just" hedonic either, but even more basic; it is the desire for life, and life is relationship with the other. Ingesting food, that is, assimilating energy for maintaining biological balance and the functioning of the metabolic processes, thus means to desire, in a full and complete sense.

In the mid-nineteenth century another German philosopher, the well-known Ludwig Feuerbach, formulated a thought that has become almost a platitude in everyday language, but is hardly ever used by philosophers—"*Der Mensch ist, was er isst*" ("Man is what he eats"). The phrase is a play on words that only works in German, between the verb *sein*, "to be," and the verb *essen*, "to eat," which sound the same in the third-person singular. The statement appeared in a review of the treatise *Lehre der Nahrungsmittel für das Volk* (The theory of nutrition for the people) by the Dutch physician and physiologist Jacob Moleschott. In this work, Moleschott tried to explain the importance of eating and drinking for human beings in terms of psychophysical units on a materialist base. Feuerbach pointed out that the treatise provided philosophy with the tools for overcoming the Platonic, idealistic, and dualistic assumptions about reality, and that food provided the most important theoretical argument for proving the bond of mind and body on a scientific basis. Although Feuerbach's suggestion remained largely ignored by the Western *episteme* (Shapin 1998), it nonetheless shows that sometimes even philosophy has recognized the centrality of food, without falling back on elevation strategies. Again, the crucial issue here is to go beyond—or rather to deconstruct—the opposition between nature and culture. Food is even *philosophically* important *before* its fragmentation into social, anthropological, historical, economical domains, and the like, because food expresses a primary aesthetic (in the sense of *aisthesis*) input. On the one hand, "man is what he eats" asserts the impossibility of reducing food to a purely immaterial good; on the other—and here lies the kernel of my argument—eating (*essen*) does not totally correspond to enjoying or even tasting the food being eaten. The two perceptual experiences are different, as is easily observable from the point of view of the eater—from the "knowing from the inside" perspective we assumed from the beginning of this essay. According to our experiential and ecological approach, perceiving food does not correspond to perceiving the taste of food. These two different modes of perception represent different possibilities or *affordances* because of the *ecological relationships* between the human being qua organism (not a "higher being by divine right endowed with taste"), the food object qua additional organic system, and the context in which this relationship happens. If we accept this paradigm, the ontological hierarchy between taste and nourishment is rejected and, along the same line, the paradoxical and misleading position that tries to elevate food to the realm of "immaterial culture" is rejected. The political purposes of this elevation are clear and understandable: they intend to protect and value food cultures, against the risk of their collapse into mere material necessity. At the same time, we should also consider the reciprocal risk. Think of UNESCO 2010 awarding the status of "intangible" World Heritage to certain food "categories" such as the Mediterranean diet and French cuisine, *because* they are immaterial goods. Just as culture is not the spirit *above* the body, taste (that is, good taste, cultivation, the mark of civilization) is not *above* nourishment. The "essence" of food consists in its *being for* consumption and all that remains is the continually renewed relationship we have with it, in the great chain of energy transformation that unites biological, chemical, and physical facts, together with psychic and social facts.

I would now like to propose a pun. Let's reverse the famous and immaterialist phrase coined by Bishop Berkeley at the beginning of the eighteenth century, "esse est percipi" ("to be is to be perceived"), making it "*essen* (to eat in German) non est percipi" a principle that asserts the irreducible materiality of food. The pun then should mean: eating does not correspond to the act of being perceived, in the sense of *being tasted*. If in the last chapter I argued that dressed taste coincided with a "going toward" the food experience in a deliberate and alert fashion, gustatory indifference confronts us instead with another situation altogether. Of course, food is *also* symbolic as well as an object of imagination; try *not* eating while thinking about it or imagining it, or while writing or talking about it. You will easily notice that it won't satiate you. (When someone who prepares food does not eat it and insists on being satisfied only by cooking it, at times that person is only expressing a request for deferral—to eat later, when the tension has waned—and at other times she might actually be sated, but due to the satiety caused by the olfactory and aromatic stimuli that energized her while preparing the food.) In any case, it is unlikely that Bishop Berkeley had bread or fruit in mind when he formulated his thesis on the nonexistence of material objects and the independent existence of ideas! Irony aside, food really provides insurmountable evidence of the existence of an external world independent of our concepts, ideas, and paradigms, and this is maybe a reason that helps us understand why it has been excluded from most philosophical reflections; edible matter disturbs us because it is irreducible to any colonization by the mind. Beyond the crude spiritualism that refers to the possibility of a spirit that would not need matter, more sensible and sophisticated versions also need to be questioned. They distinguish between the level of "manifest" and ordinary perception and the level of testable scientific reality. Some of these positions, like the one proposed in the second half of the twentieth century by the American philosopher Wilfrid Sellars, offer a differentiation between the level of ordinary and sensitive experience, erected by way of conceptual schemes, and the level of scientific proof, grounded in scientifically proven theories. The first level corresponds to the perception of a table or an apple in front of us, the second one states that in front of us there is "really" neither a table nor an apple, but an accumulation of subatomic particles or of molecules with certain bonds and a certain spatial collocation. According to this theory, the "manifest image" of the world is "apparent" with respect to the second one, the "scientific image." We can translate that debate to our issues: a link is possible with respect to the ideology of nutritionism, in which a food is nothing more than a compound of substances—a position that has led some people to think that it is possible to be fed directly through pills containing everything the body needs. It is widely known that such experiments were attempted with astronauts in space in the 1960s and 1970s, as well as with professional athletes, and the results were negative. Millions of years of evolution have literally made foodstuffs *indispensable* to us in their complete, full, and manifest materiality, in their concrete *solidity*, *not* just their components. And one must add—although this does not directly affect our topic—that the same holds for the tables and chairs in front of us. The great scientific projects involving the *reduction* of reality to a few simple essential components have all failed, leaving it to philosophical theories and scientific programs to understand and explain the *complexity* instead. This is a key point for the wonderful problem of perception in general and for a food aesthetics in particular, because it undermines the nutritionist objection: the experience of food is not the experience of its components. We do not perceive molecules, but food, *even when* we don't eat it attentively.

The indifference to taste must now be placed in this theoretical framework. Normally, we eat and drink using perceptive capacities variable in intensity and attention according to the circumstances. In some cases, the level of attention is so low that it does not elicit an explicit gustatory intentionality, a "focus" on taste as such. Many everyday attitudes concerning food are characterized by what Walter Benjamin called, as we already mentioned, "reception in distraction." Clearly, this is not an apology for indifference. The aesthetics of taste promotes the value of gastronomy and the attention to the cultivation of taste, through pleasure and knowledge. But since it does so while taking into account the environmental variations according to the ecological situation, it is right to integrate pleasure and knowledge into the general flow in which such devices emerge and develop. John Dewey illustrates this clearly: "We have *an* experience when the material experienced runs its course to fulfillment. Then and then only is it integrated within and demarcated in the general stream of experience. . . . Such an experience is a whole and carries with it its own individualizing quality and self-sufficiency. It is *an* experience. . . . For life is no uniform uninterrupted march or flow. It is a thing of histories . . . each with its own unrepeated quality pervading it throughout" (1980, 35–36). Dewey wants to emphasize the difference between the aesthetic experience and its indiscriminate flow, but within a continuous chain: if the aesthetic experience grows, it is because there is a vital flow, some kind of background material that makes its growth possible. As a follow-up to the Deweyan idea, we can see indifference to taste as a particular kind of *history*: On the one hand, it does not belong to the indiscriminate flow of the vital process, since it emerges because eating requires a deliberate suspension of other activities. On the other hand, it still does not rise to the aesthetic experience of taste, but perhaps instead to an aesthetics of hunger. However, if indifference can express, as is often the case, chronic apathy, laziness, a general lack of critical perspective, and the passive lowering of standards, if it can refer to the infectious anonymity of *private* lives—private comes from the Latin *privus*, "lacking"—it is just as true that it can also have different and opposite meanings, and even play with the qualitative amplification of the experience as such (there is, in fact, a *taste of indifference* or, in the words of Baudelaire, a *taste of nothing*).

For all those reasons, the attitude of gustatory indifference is difficult to address explicitly. In fact, finding appropriate examples has not been easy.

Contingent Indifference

The first chapter of Don DeLillo's short novel *The Body Artist* describes the Sunday morning breakfast of the film director Rey and his wife Lauren, a young performance artist. The dialogue is sparse. The atmosphere is rarefied and distressing and sets the stage for what will follow: Rey's suicide and Lauren's elaboration of grief through hallucinations. In this text, food is not addressed as such, but in the first chapter, DeLillo describes the small everyday actions involved in lovingly preparing breakfast: coffee, cereal, tea, blueberries, honey, butter, toast. This very short but extraordinary passage marks the growing tension: "She took a bite of cereal and *forgot to taste it*. She lost the taste somewhere between the time she put the food in her mouth and the regretful second she swallowed it" (2001, 19, my emphasis). This striking remark describes an action of Lauren's. A reflection by the narrator on reading the Sunday morning papers, an action that leads to imaginary conversations with the characters in those articles, precedes that moment, "until you become aware you are doing it and then you stop, seeing whatever is in front of you at the time, like half a glass of juice in your husband's hand" (19). What does Lauren's forgetfulness express? The care and attention put into preparing breakfast set the stage for its meaning; we are faced with a *contingent distraction*, a sudden and nondeliberate inattention within the experiential flow. The perceptual attention to taste retreats for a few seconds because a new detail requires attention, yet with a lingering feeling of regret. The cereal is swallowed and its flavor is lost beyond recovery. Contingent distraction is a very common case of gustatory indifference in everyday life. It is not something to condemn, but to understand. The frequency of food intake, which rhythmically marks the course of our days, includes the possibility of distraction from the *quality* of the substances. In all these cases, the perceptual experience is not aesthetic, yet it would be wrong to underestimate its importance.

Marcel Proust, the narrator par excellence, offers another telling example. It may seem bizarre to include Proust in this chapter on indifference, seeing that the French writer has become an eponym for great attention to food experiences, thanks to the well-known episode of the *petites madeleines*, the cakes that deliver extraordinary pleasure connected to childhood memories. To compensate for what might seem an insult, therefore, I will first quote the more famous excerpt, not only because it is so beautiful that it deserves to be read over and over again, but also because it will give further incentive to the reversal of perspective that follows. Here then the passage from *Swann's Way*:

> When one day in winter, as I came home, my mother, seeing that I was cold, suggested that, contrary to my habit, I have a little tea. I refused at first and then, I do not know why, changed my mind. She sent for one of those squat, plump cakes called "petites madeleines" that look as though they have been molded in the grooved valve of a scallop-shell. And soon, mechanically oppressed by the gloomy day and the prospect of a sad future, I carried to my lips a spoonful of tea in which I had let soften a piece of *Madeleine*. But at the very instant when the mouthful of tea mixed with cake-crumbs touched my palate, I quivered, attentive to the extraordinary thing that was happening to me. A delicious pleasure *invaded* me, *isolated* me, without my having any notion as to its cause. It had immediately made the vicissitudes of life *unimportant* to me, its disasters innocuous, its brevity illusory, acting in the same way that love acts, by filling me with a precarious essence. . . . Where could it have come to me from— this powerful joy? I sensed that it was connected to the taste of the tea and the cake, but that it went infinitely far beyond it, could not be of the same nature. Where did it come from? What did it mean? How could I grasp it? I drink a second mouthful, in which I find nothing more than in the first, a third that give me

a little less than the second. It is time for me to stop, the virtue of the drink seems to be diminishing. It is clear that the truth I am seeking is not in the drink, but in me. The drink has awoken it in me, but does not know that truth, and cannot do more that repeat indefinitely, with less and less force, this same testimony which I do not know how to interpret and which I want at least to be able to ask of it again and find again, intact, available to me, soon, for a decisive clarification. I put down the cup and turn to my mind. It is up to me to find the truth. But how? . . . I go back in my thoughts to the moment when I took the first spoonful of tea. I find the same state, without any new clarity. I ask my mind to make another effort, to bring back one more the sensation that is slipping away. . . . Then for a second time I create an empty space before it, I confront it again with the still recent taste that first mouthful and I feel something quiver in me, shift, try to rise, *something* that seems to have been unanchored at a great depth; I do not know what it is, but it comes up slowly; I feel the resistance and I hear the murmur of the distances traversed. . . . And suddenly the memory appeared. That taste was the taste of the little piece of *madeleine* which in Sunday mornings at Combray (because that day I did not go out before it was time for Mass), when I went to say good morning to her in her bedroom, my Aunt Léonie would give me after dipping it in her infusion of tea or lime-blossom. (2003b, 47–49, my emphasis)

This passage could be (and has been) the subject of endless comments, but we have to limit ourselves to the essential concerns. The gustatory pleasure that invades Marcel closely resembles the totalizing and pervasive experience that we have already come across in the selections from Amélie Nothomb, even though Proust adds a detail useful for our present purposes. Of the explosion of that pleasure, he writes, "it had immediately made the vicissitudes of life *unimportant* to me, its disasters innocuous, its brevity illusory." In that scene, in that specific context of the experience, taste becomes the main character banishing all the rest to indifference, to the anonymous and undifferentiated buzz that is the background of every vital process.

Quite surprisingly, then, in another section of the novel Proust gives us a totally different description of an experience with food: in the face of a strong emotional investment (falling in love with Gilberte) and turbulence, which absorbs all of his perceptual attention, taste is relegated to the background of the undifferentiated. We are in the first part of *In the Shadow of Young Girls in Flower* and Marcel, recalling an afternoon spent at the Swann's home, writes: "[Gilberte] even asked me what time my parents dined, as though I knew something about it, as though the emotional upset from which I was suffering could enable any sensation such as lack of appetite or hunger, any notion of dinner or family, to survive in my *vacant* memory and *paralysed stomach*. Unfortunately this paralysis was only temporary; and there would come a time when cakes which I consumed without noticing them would have to be digested. But that moment was still in the future; and in the present, Gilberte made '*my tea*.' I drank huge quantities of it, although normally a single cup of tea would keep me awake for twenty-four hours. So it was that my mother had come to remark, 'It's a worry—as sure as that boy goes to the Swann's— he comes home sick.' But while I was at the Swann's—I would have been unable to say *whether or not it was really tea* I was drinking. *And even if I had known, I would have gone on drinking it*; for even if I had been restored momentarily to proper awareness of the present, this would not have given me back the ability to remember the past or foresee the future" (2003a, 81–82, my emphasis). This passage masterfully describes the loss of appetite, but most of all the gustatory indifference that marks intense emotional states. We have already come across the connection between taste and emotion, but it was manifest in the opposite experience. In Calvino's *Under the Jaguar Sun*, Olivia and the narrator, on vacation in Mexico, explored the country and communicated with each other through taste. The quality of such taste perception, attentive and intense, all-encompassing and sophisticated—more generally, the "passion for food," as it is quite tellingly called—is very common in long-term relationships, to seal, modify, enhance, or sometimes even exalt stagnant sentimental dynamics. The experience described by Proust, whose character is usually so attentive to the sensory and sensitive nuances of every vital element (even the food-related ones: Gilberte continues to prepare him "his tea" because Marcel has *his own tea*, a tea to his taste, as all tea enthusiasts have), is therefore particularly significant. The contingent indifference is a suspension of attention, an involuntary paralysis of taste, just as it was for the performance artist Lauren, even though for different reasons. The point is that both attitudes are relevant, appropriate, and consistent with the overall ecology of the experience in which they grow and develop. Try imagining the comic, grotesque, and pathetic effect of a scene in which perceptual dynamics based on an evident emotional or sentimental situation persist. Think, for example, of a first date between two people in love, in which the distraction from the object of affection in favor of a dish or a wine was to cause inappropriate behavior. Or even—leaving our field, but with an example that, I think, hits the spot—think of the same distraction in favor of a ball game. This explains why so many women are disappointed by male attitudes whose objects of attention shift after the initial phase of falling in love. Unfortunately, this is not something done deliberately, because the objects of attention vary according to changes in emotional investment. If one objected that I am working here with a rigid definition of "appropriateness" and that I am using context as a regulatory term, I would reply that appropriate is what every *single* experience finds to be appropriate, and this is not an a priori condition, but rather the outcome of processes that develop in a field of forces.

Compulsive Indifference and Atmospheric Indifference

A different kind of gustatory indifference can be found in an early story by Italo Calvino, "Theft in a Pastry Shop." It is the story of three poor petty criminals, in the starving postwar Italy of the last century, who one night rob a bakery. While the gang leader—dubbed Dritto (that is, Clever)—does not care about the wide array of sweets they find in the shop, the other two, Gesubambino and Uora-uora, cannot resist the temptation to gorge themselves on pastries, cakes, sugar, and candied fruit, thus jeopardizing the outcome of the robbery. Having just climbed in through the window, Gesubambino "flung himself at the shelves, choking himself with cakes, cramming two or three inside his mouth at a time, *without even tasting them*" (Calvino 1984, 100, my emphasis). In this scene, the indifference is the unintended and almost paradoxical result of such a violent impulse for the cake merely as a sweet item, such that it becomes undifferentiated and produces the loss of flavor. It is a *compulsive indifference* that can be caused by factors such as hunger or, in contrast, too much food. How many people do not taste anything anymore because they have already had everything and have tasted too much before? Here we have a very different kind of relationship with food from the one presented with Amélie Nothomb's novels. Also there, in fact, the encounter with food led to an experience that focused only on one quality of the object, its being sweet, but the sweet encounter provoked intense pleasure and not undifferentiated assimilation. Of course, these different experiences can be explained in reference to the different contexts: whereas the three poor thieves of Calvino's story are, in fact, destitute and hungry, Amélie is at home in a rich and comfortable environment and hunger is of no or little importance to her gustatory experience.

One might wonder about the extent to which indifference can be seen as an aesthetic experience. Until now, I have argued that taste experience is aesthetic in two distinct senses: the first inherent in hedonic impulse and pleasure variously declined, and the second inherent in knowledge as an intentionally acted upon perception. Both cases give rise to a multiplicity of performances and satisfying relationships. I called these systemic structures aesthetic relationships. How does indifference fit into the picture? As a matter of fact, the experience of indifference I described above is not an aesthetic experience *in the strict sense*, but rather an experience that outlines and punctuates true aesthetic relationships. In the perceptual flow of human existence, the relationship with food is undeniably dominated by experiences of indifference. For this reason, they have aesthetic legitimacy. Even in a developmental and adaptive key, it would not be possible to always maintain a high threshold of attention. Reception in distraction thus seems to be a necessary condition of the "gustatory" experience, and in many cases distraction and attention alternate within the same environmental *scenario*. Imagine, for example, being at a dinner attended by various people, some of whom are wine experts while others are not, and all meet for the first time. Everyone is sitting at the same table and, after having introduced themselves, the guests begin talking and getting to know one another. The conversation on different subjects is accompanied by the dishes and bottles of wine that receive varying attention. The experts will be more likely to perceive attentively than the nonexperts, of course, but this will also depend on their involvement in the conversation, on the level of interest generated by the food, and on other factors. Perceptual indifference is, in fact, a kind of setting, a background noise from which something can always arise, as in the phenomenon known as the "cocktail party effect." This time imagine being in a room full of people and you are talking to a friend. Suddenly, someone who is in a distant corner of the room says your name. Now your attention is captured, and you might be surprised to have caught your name in the middle of all that noise. The "cocktail party effect" is explained by the sciences of communication with the notion of "salience," that is, the perceptual filter that allows selectively paying attention to what emotionally or intellectually moves us (Burnham and Skilleås 2012). As becomes clear in these examples, indifference is also a useful device in ordinary ecological relationships. It is precisely for this reason that it is necessary to locate and understand this attitude with respect to the acts of eating; in everyday life, feelings or perceptions are rarely exclusive.

Here are two more examples to illustrate with new nuances the picture outlined above. The first comes from another contemporary American writer, Chuck Palahniuk, notable for a phenomenological and amoral attitude toward his characters and for his ability to avoid any distance between the everyday and the exceptional. In his novels this often takes on monstrous, unhealthy, and borderline features. A passage from his fifth novel, titled *Lullaby* and part of a series (together with *Haunted* and *Diary*) that the author has called a "trilogy of horror," sums up a context where food plays an essentially mechanical function and gustatory perception has no chance of emerging: "Nash is eating a bowl of chili. He's at a back table in the bar on Third Avenue. The bartender is slumped forward on the bar, his arms still swinging above the barstools. . . . Somebody in a greasy apron is face down on the grill among greasy hamburgers. . . . And Nash looks up, chili red around his mouth, and says: 'I thought you'd like a little privacy for this.' . . . He digs the spoon into the bowl of chili. He puts the spoon in his mouth and says, 'And don't lecture me about the evils of necrophilia.' He says, 'You're about the last person who can give that lecture.' His mouth full of chili, Nash says, 'I know who you are.' He swallows and says, 'You're still wanted for questioning.' He licks the chili smeared around his lips and says, 'I saw your wife's death certificate.' He smiles and says, 'Signs of postmortem sexual intercourse?' . . . 'You can't kill me,' Nash says. He crumbles a handful of crackers into his bowl and says, 'You and me, we're exactly alike' . . . Nash jabs his spoon around in the crackers and red and says, 'You killing me would be the same as you killing yourself.' I say, shut up. 'Relax,' he says. 'I didn't give nobody a letter about this.' Nash crunches a mouthful of crackers and red. 'That would've been stupid,' he says. 'I mean, think.' And he shovels in more chili" (Palahniuk 2002, 233–35).

This dialogue takes place in a bar where the narrator, the reporter Carl Streator, discovers some uncomfortable truths about a physician, John Nash, a necrophiliac murderer. During the confession, Nash is constantly eating. The continuous assimilation of food marks the rhythm of the story but no gustatory perception ever comes into play. Taste simply does not exist here. This attitude of indifference corresponds neither to contingent distraction as seen in the novel by DeLillo nor to the compulsive indifference in Calvino's story, but to something that could be defined as *atmospheric indifference*: the characters' emotional states and behavior are swallowed up by a neutral and contagious environment that absorbs and discolors everything. The meal is consumed at a crime scene, and this is not without importance; in any case, a salient gustatory perception would seem inappropriate and out of place in this context. The entire novel is permeated by this atmospheric quality, and this is of exemplary interest here.

The work of Palahniuk is exemplary also with respect to a certain type of food habit. It is no coincidence that the chili and hamburgers mentioned in the text represent typical ordinary food that is better suited to careless and distracted consumption than to dedicated and refined perceptions. In Palahniuk's fiction food is often used in an "antigastronomic" relation, as we can see in his most famous novel, *Choke*, in which the main character, Victor, stages numerous choking episodes in restaurants in order to obtain the money necessary to care for his sick mother from the customers who save him and are touched by his circumstances. But *Lullaby* also contains references to food that go in a controversial direction. An exchange between a character called Oyster and Carl Streator is particularly interesting. Oyster is an orthorexic: he professes a militant and ethical attitude to taste, because he is a vegetarian who pays attention to the quality of food and its impact on the economy and society. "To me, Oyster says, 'The only power of life and death you have is every time you order a hamburger at McDonald's.' His face stuck in my face, he says, 'You just pay your filthy money and somewhere else, the ax falls'" (100). In the discussion, the narrator defends a point of view much more in line with the novel's poetics and claims the right to a naked, uncritical, and even willfully ignorant pleasure: "Oyster and his tree-hugging, eco-bullshit, his bio-invasive, apocryphal bullshit. The virus of his information. . . . After listening to Oyster, a glass of milk isn't just a nice drink with chocolate chip cookies. It's cows forced to stay pregnant and pumped with hormones" (157–58). This case illustrates another aspect of food attitudes: laying claim to a noncultivated and uncritical pleasure that develops on the inside of atmospheric indifference. On closer inspection, this approach seems to correspond largely to the mass food habits in our society: the removal of any care and attention to food—from production to eating—due to disaffection brought about by too much food. The ensuing pattern of enjoyment related to the product as a pure *commodity*, cheap and easy, always available, does not ask for any effort (note Streator's contempt, in the passage quoted above, for the "virus of his information"). This has nothing to do with the naked pleasure that surprises and promotes change, psychic evolution, and meaningful relationships. In that case, the lack of information was part of an experience oriented to deepening enjoyment, restoring it to childhood strength. Something completely different takes place in these scenes, where the characters do not contemplate the taste of food as a device for creative exploration.

The atmospheric indifference to taste can emerge in still different contexts, where food plays a fundamental role as an instrument of quality performances associated with the body and its public representation, particularly in sports (bodybuilders and professional athletes, but also amateurs) as well as fashion and the entertainment industry (models, actors and actresses, public "faces"). Often in these experiences the approach to food is merely nutritionist. Eating is seen as the pure assimilation of substances and food is consumed—occasionally together with supplements and nutraceuticals—with great care with respect to its elementary quantities, but with total indifference to its taste (Parasecoli 2005). Eating becomes extremely important as a vector of the body's desired development, in terms of physical appearance. In a seemingly paradoxical manner, however, here food is purely vicarious, it is subject to a "Promethean" determination that utilizes it at will, it does not benefit from the assignment of any value in itself and is wrongly believed not to have the least effect on the processes of pleasure, knowledge, and intellectual happiness. In this particular situation, atmospheric indifference to "gusto" becomes the apology of an instrumental and dualistic conception. The body, which is merely an external representation of "beauty" as appearance and adherence to the paradigms of a social consensus in use in a given context, needs food. The psychic and emotional interiority activated by the enjoyment of taste is removed with often devastating consequences.

THE NEUTRAL

The analysis of the modes of access to gustatory indifference brought to light numerous variants. However, they all have one common trait: indifferent experience to taste lies within an anonymous backdrop, a "generalized buzz" in which the foodstuff loses the sharpness of its qualitative outlines and turns into neutral matter. The category of the neutral has attracted the attention of many philosophers. The neutral is the expression of an elusive experience, very difficult to grasp and to define. For our subject, it is enough to recall two main interpretative lines, one that sees the neutral as a "horizon of meaning" indispensable to perception and even to living (this is the position of the French philosopher Maurice Blanchot), and one that sees it as a specific and historical determination of thought, provisional and to be overcome (although for different reasons, this idea was proposed by philosophers such as Emmanuel Lévinas and Luce Irigaray). Our perspective runs transversally across these two options, for in aesthetics of taste as relation all experiences have multiple possibilities and, consequently, they may express different values. Gustatory indifference is no exception. As the examples above have shown, there are cases of perfectly fitting and appropriate indifference, but also cases that manifest incoherent and deficient attitudes. Regarding food, we cannot endorse the idea that indifferent neutrality is the highest experience, because that would mean refusing the aesthetics of taste as the environmental perception of differences that promotes the capability of enjoying quality, through experiences of pleasure as well as functional and formed knowledge. At the same time, we cannot endorse the idea that—to put it bluntly—without tasting there is no eating. To give an example. The Belgian philosopher Luce Irigaray argued, in a book with the same title, that "to speak is never neutral," meaning that language and thought are outcomes of gender, theoretical constructs oriented by the constructors' gender. In particular, Irigaray declared—thus presupposing that knowledge is the result of conflicts of forces, and then the expression of the prevalent power—that Western thought and language constituted themselves through male categories from which the founding hierarchies of classical philosophy derive. She mentions the advantage of theory over practice, of reason over passion, of the distal senses over the proximal senses (Irigaray 1985). The argument raised by Irigaray benefits our discussion regarding taste and gastronomy. Do they express gender rules? It is difficult to deny completely. But if, to paraphrase the title of Irigaray's book, we were to ask whether "eating is ever neutral," we could not give an answer in absolute terms. The relationship between food, cooking, taste, and gender cannot be denied; and this also explains the subordinate nature of home cooking as mainly women's business, and the ennoblement of "artistic" gastronomy and cuisine as mainly men's business, but that is another story I cannot tell here. However, the subject I propose here is not limited to this specific determination of the perceptual experience of food.

Observation shows us foods that lead to less marked gustatory approaches. These foods develop less oriented experiences, that is, experiences less committed to cultural taste and perhaps even to less intense pleasure, and more commensurate instead to experiencing the neutral. The most basic and simple foods such as water, bread, milk, wild herbs, and so on are of that kind. Obviously, I am not suggesting that these foods are without taste; neither do I claim these foods to be "simple" in ontological terms. Making good bread is anything but simple, and eating good bread can be a wonderful gustatory experience. When I write "simple" I refer to the perceiver's perspective in terms of taste experiences. In other words, I only want to point out the greater propensity some foods possess for entering into a less oriented and marked relationship than other foods such as wine or fine dining creations *usually* require. Please mind the italics; my aim is to remind us of the environmental occurrences of eating and tasting. Generally the qualitative parameters of taste are intensity, strength, flavor complexity, and their subsequent elaborations. It is within *this* grammar of taste that the paradigm of gastronomy as value and culture has grown. A "new gastronomy," however, stemming from an aesthetics of food as an ecological experience, can accept the challenge of *also* embracing a less intense, less powerful, less complex taste in its domain. Let's take water as maybe the most relevant example. According to the Chinese sage *Laozi*, water comes closest to the "way," the *tao* (Jullien 1998). Water recalls neutrality as the background of immanence, as the possibility of life itself. On the dietary level, it refers to gustatory indifference, not because it cannot express different aesthetic and nonaesthetic properties—qualitative differences in waters regarding both chemical composition and sensory perception do exist—but rather as the vital element par excellence, the main component of our bodies and of the entire ecological system in which life on earth appeared. In a phenomenological sense, water easily induces an inattentive perception—remember "reception in distraction"—that does not focus on qualitative nuances. Water attracts an indifferent and nonaesthetic perception. In this sense, it is the exact opposite of wine, even if Barthes suggested the historically correct opposition of wine and milk, two liquids that have never been mixed. The recent fashion of water-tasting courses along the lines of wine-tasting courses was a bit of a stretch, and explains the reason for their failure, just as the existence of "water menus" in some gourmet restaurants often elicits indifference. If wine is a strongly culturalized artifact, the expression of choices and styles, as well as a dispensable adult beverage, considering water in the same way and turning it into a matter of *expertise* and specific knowledge really seem irrelevant, by comparison, in most daily experiences— maybe even an offense to sensitivity. No one feels ignorant or inadequate for not being "proficient" in the taste of water. Only with a focused and finalized perceptive effort could we prepare ourselves for the gustatory and qualitative description of water in everyday circumstances. Again, this is not always true and de jure: there can be specific occurrences in which we realize the bad taste of one water or the good taste of another. And of course, this argument does not apply to professionals in water analysis for health, hygiene, or sales and marketing reasons. They have a different scope and another perceptive project.

The above reasoning does not underestimate water, rather the opposite. Water is a primary pleasure and can also be great when we are dehydrated. But the typology of this pleasure is different from that of wine or adult foods; it is a more neutral pleasure and less prone to specific attention. The pleasure of water is normally a *haptic* pleasure, having to do with lips, throat, and tissues and only occasionally the recognition of specific flavors. Similar considerations that should always be evaluated case by case with respect to every single experience lived and to every single ecological perception may apply to "simple" and "basic" foods that refer to the deeper biological stratum of human evolution, such as milk, grains, and some vegetables.

An original elaboration of Chinese thought can be found in the philosophy of the French sinologist François Jullien. He developed an aesthetics of taste based on the category of *blandness* (Jullien 2007), which has some points in common with the perspective of indifference I propose here. According to Jullien, the bland (which in his system does not correspond to the neutral, but for our purposes we can ignore this difference) indicates the overcoming of every single radical inclination and is a kind of equalizer of all flavors expressed in its midst, where they stop opposing one another. In this sense, blandness is the most difficult "flavor" to perceive, because it is a backdrop, a vague, rarified, and faded sensation and its paradigm is water. As I have already mentioned, the grammar of Western gastronomy—a Eurocentric, Mediterranean-centric, even Francocentric grammar until a few years ago—has instead been strongly bent on depreciating every "bland" perception, which is neither intense nor strong or complex. The Western gastronomic model is that of variety, diversity, and intensity. Whatever does not fit in it is usually considered less "interesting" and less "complex," and, into this context, whatever is "less" converges on the neutral and its experiential relative, indifference. In *Under the Jaguar Sun*, "bland" was the epithet that Olivia used for her husband, accusing him of being incapable of feeling life's nuances strongly and powerfully. (In Italian, when something does not interest us, or we are not passionate about it, we say that it is "tasteless.") However, in the contemporary adventures of dressed taste, it is possible to come across a different and freer paradigm, in keeping with a more comprehensive evaluation of the neutral. In recent years, some new trends in fine cuisine and cooking seem to be moving in this direction with simpler dishes, easier ways of tasting them, and a more "relaxed" approach even to fine dining.

I feel that it is important to repeat once more that such a theoretical framework is not a defense of the neutral or the bland tout court; instead, it provides a clarification of the experiential *potential* that might originate from the neutral and the bland in given contexts.

In fact, the neutral often expresses the ideology of nutritionism: supplements and functional foods that have neutral taste since their synthesized components are without flavor. And this ideology is in turn tied to food production of very poor quality that delivers almost tasteless foods, badly grown or bred to minimize costs and maximize profits. Thus, in many cases indifference and neutrality do not represent an opportunity to be seized, most obviously with the expression of production and taste standardization. The aesthetics of taste as an ecological relationship therefore suggests paying careful attention and discussing each case individually.

THE EXTENSION OF PLEASURE AND THE LIMITS OF GUSTATORY EXCLUSIVISM

The considerations regarding water and the neutral lead to the development of a broader meaning of pleasure. The pleasure I presented in the first chapter had a strong characterization in terms of inclination and exclusion since when the main reference is intensity some flavors exclude others. A different pleasure, though, is also possible. A pleasure experienced *around* food and not *of* food, that is, one where food can play the role of a supporting actor. It is appropriate to insert this kind of pleasure into the framework of the indifferent approach, for at this point, it will be easier to understand its legitimacy. Imagine a very common situation. You decide to go out for dinner with some friends and choose the place for reasons other than the quality of the meal, such as the beauty of the location, the people who frequent it, the friendliness of the owners, excellent live music, the convenience regarding the fact that afterward you may want to go see a movie. For a negotiated and deliberate reason, in one of these or other possible cases one decides to subordinate gustatory experience—in terms of both naked pleasure and dressed taste—to another overriding enjoyment, within which considerations of taste are then subsumed. Experiences like the one just described are perfectly legitimate, and they show once again the complexity and variability of our relationship with food. Loading all the weight of possible pleasure *around* the taste *of* food is, in fact, at best a naive and often very limiting attitude, which even runs the risk of missing the overall understanding of the ongoing experience.

In the second chapter, I mentioned the possibility of broadening gustatory pleasure through cultural awareness and the acquisition of expertise. Remember the words of Wendell Berry and Bertrand Russell; knowing more about the history of food, about its sources and criteria of production and so on orients and intensifies pleasure. Sometimes this is true. With respect to different cases, I have now arrived at the argument that the acquisition of knowledge is not sufficient, or more precisely, that "acquiring" is not the right term to be applied here. Since this point will be discussed more thoroughly in the next chapter, I will only highlight here that what we need is not an extension of the pleasure *of* food, but rather *around* food; occasionally, one can skillfully reduce the importance of (the taste of) food. With respect to this approach, which I propose to call "taste exclusivism," the attitude of someone who thinks they have to appreciate food only and exclusively through taste appreciation, there are then at least two limitations. The first limitation has to do with the social nature of taste. If taste has an eminently social and mundane dimension, it becomes necessary to emphasize its necessarily discrete and intermittent essence. It is impossible to savor and taste *in continuum* because our physiological apparatus cannot bear it, and also because we are not always together with others. The gustatory experience requires complementary moments—respites, reprieves, and frequent breaks. It is certainly possible to eat on one's own and this is often associated today with the atmospheric indifference that characterizes entire lifestyles and behavior patterns. It is even possible to relish a lone meal, as experts, critics, and food professionals sometimes do, *tasting* in solitude. But this practice often goes hand in hand with specific purposes and does not represent the ordinary and common model of the experience of taste, which, not by chance, requires sharing. Sampling is not eating, tasting wine is not drinking it, and there is nothing more evident than socialization to make this difference clear. Sampling and tasting are activities that cry out for concentration, and maybe even a certain amount of solitude. But how many people enjoy intentionally going to a restaurant alone, or opening a bottle of wine on their own? Again, I do not pose this question in order to establish an alternative rule; it depends. For example, wine tasting is a special case, due to the very nature of the object being storable. Wine allows repeated interruptions of the taste relationship within the same experience. For this reason, it could come close to a kind of quasi-illusion of suspension of the temporal dimension. It is, in fact, possible to drink a bottle of wine very slowly and for many hours, approaching that meditative and almost contemplative state typical of other experiences that we are easily willing to accept as aesthetic, because of the prevalent paradigm of visual perception based on contemplation (Scruton 2010). But this is not the case for most of our everyday experiences, in which taste, above all, develops in a relationship that includes communicative expression. From the mother/child relationship during nursing, to the apprenticeship that characterizes the establishment of a grammar of taste in adulthood, which takes place in social contexts, gustatory perception misses the necessity of solitary experiences. Generally speaking, expressions of pleasure and appreciation require community and witnesses. Even Michel de Montaigne wrote that no pleasure has any savor without communication. If, on the one hand, taste exclusivism forgets to place the experience of taste in its broadest context, and therefore neglects the possibilities resulting from the extension of pleasure, on the other it does not sufficiently consider that the taste experience should *in any case* be a limited experience confined in space and time.

The second limit of taste exclusivism has to do precisely with the specific nature of the temporal structure of the taste relationship. Tasting is a rhythmic temporal experience with rather narrow and hardly expandable boundaries. In comparison with other aesthetic experiences—such as writing, reading, looking at that famous painting, meditating under a tree—eating, due to its process made of ingestion, digestion, metabolism, does not allow the perception of time annihilation (Telfer 1996). Even if we were experiencing the most intense pleasure, tasting the most wonderful food in an exceptional restaurant, we would be dealing with an active temporal consciousness, at least in the sense that, at some point, if we were to exceed the food intake our body would send us strong and clear signals. Think of the gastric torture of many wedding banquets or other rituals, where the time for food consumption is extended above and beyond any reasonable limit. This saturation signal is certainly also noticeable with other experiences, but in a different sense (one cannot get drunk by reading, writing, or meditating) and with much wider boundaries. It is possible to "get lost" in thought, imagination, and fantasy, while meditating under a tree for hours or looking at Botticelli's *Primavera*. Taste does not grant such possibilities, and it is for this reason that frequent ennoblings of the taste experience in fine modern arts pertain to *memory* and memories—from Proust's madeleines to countless other examples from literature.

This limit leads me to underline again a crucial point. In traditional aesthetics, aesthetic pleasure is associated with a certain idea of duration, based on the (visual) paradigm of contemplation from a distance. Instead, in gustatory aesthetics as a relational and ecological aesthetic, pleasure and enjoyment are considered to be aesthetic, but they depend on a different paradigm. One must free the aesthetic pleasure from the notion of duration modeled on visual contemplation and connect it to a *haptic* relationship. The aesthetic pleasure of food is a vital, interactive, and basically short pleasure bounded by a period of contact. Therefore, the second limit mentioned above does not involve a differentiation between aesthetic and nonaesthetic pleasures. It instead emphasizes the fact that human beings require different types of aesthetic pleasure, those pertaining to contemplation and distance, and those pertaining to physical involvement, proximity, and physical engagement.

The Wisdom of Taste, the Taste of Wisdom

If you make your pleasure depend on drinking good wine,
you condemn yourself to the pain of sometimes drinking bad wine.
We must have a less exacting and freer taste.
—MONTAIGNE

Wisdom is not an additional access to the experience of food, but the ability to recognize and understand the emergence, the relevance, or the presence of each of the three described modes of access from a refined, comprehensive, and aware perception. From the arguments I proposed in this essay, this kind of perception can be called an aesthetic perception, and it corresponds to a *savoir-faire*, a knowing how to move in the world, a way of possessing characteristics such as *flexibility*, *regulation*, and *transition*.

The route traveled thus far has described particular inclinations in the gustatory relationship. The experience of pleasure insisted on the capacity to *receive*, to be available and permeable to naked and naive delight, a kind of rewarding passivity. The experience of knowledge was proposed, in contrast, as a *moving toward*, a meeting with food through its most varied qualitative pleats. A dressed taste, the result of an active, cultivated, and adult approach. The experience of indifference, then, was characterized not only in terms of deprivation and deficiency, but as a *withdrawal* of gustatory attention from the foreground, a feeling of more or less enduring extraneousness, brought about for different reasons and directed at the emergence of other experiential projects. I repeatedly pointed out that those three ways of access to food, presented as separate in the architecture of this essay, in reality intertwine, overlap, and reshape themselves. In one's life, situations are almost never clear-cut and separate; most of the time, they are hybrid and therefore they ask for flexibility and adaptability. Wisdom thus does not correspond to a strict rule, but rather to a suggestion: trying to understand as many different experiences as possible in order to joyfully participate in the variety of ecological gustatory occurrences.

TASTE AND PLEASURE, EXPERIENCE, AND WISDOM

The intertwining of naked pleasure and dressed taste can be observed on many occasions. Think of the intentional re-creation of childhood taste. Many chefs are attracted to this project. In a video with the significant title *Like a Kid in a Sweetshop* posted on his restaurant's website, Heston Blumenthal of the famous restaurant The Fat Duck in Bray, England, explains to his clients how to prepare for the tasting experience that will take place in vivo, by describing with the help of a number of coworkers and scientists the processes that trigger the pleasure of food in relation to childhood memories.

Chef David Scabin of Combal Zero in Rivoli, Italy, stated in an interview in 2008, "I start from an advanced position, and that is producing taste, but I hardly take it into account anymore. Because what I try to sell here is Pleasure. . . . I have invented a system that turns pleasure into emotion. And from emotion one passes on to experience. . . . In the gastronomic field the loop between emotion and experience is fatal, because if experience resides on the conscious side, emotion is still unconscious. However, the part I am most interested in is the 'animal' one tied to pleasure. All of us enjoy, but we don't all do so in the same manner. I'm interested in this side because it is the most popular and at the same time the most true, even though there is no guarantee that I produce tastes and things that give me pleasure. The biggest problem is when the passage enters into the conscious phase, into experience, after which one can only be reexcited with difficulty. At this point, transgression and perversion come to our rescue. A well-balanced employment of them can kick-start an experience. They interrupt a schema. They reproduce pleasure. We often trivialize things that, redusted and repolished, reobtain pleasure. At times even a negative taste can be an appropriate stimulus for recreating the experience" (Scabin 2008). Scabin's words express a very high level of awareness, which permits him re-create unusual and intertwined types of experience thanks to sophisticated technique and deliberate intent. Clearly, however, nothing is less immediate or natural than a project that solicits an emotion in enjoyment by way of a stimulus offered through certain preparations. As a result, we find ourselves within the aspirations and horizons of highly structured expectations. But, as the method used in this essay suggests, in order to understand taste experiences, it is appropriate to describe them primarily from the point of view of the one who perceives them, and not only from the outside and metatheoretical vantage of the external observer and the cook. I assumed from the beginning that understanding taste as experience means above all knowing taste from the inside. Consequently, projects such as the one described above by Scabin can be seen from the perceptual side. This helps to remove the generalist and all-encompassing interpretation according to which there is further evidence for the truism that taste is "just cultural" and, instead, helps us *to live* gustatory experiences in their specificity. I argue that this is the right way to approach the subject because taste does not envisage a completely external look since it affects everybody. Thus, an experience of gustatory pleasure re-created and related to childhood memory does not correspond to an experience of childish pleasure lived directly by a child, but, in turn, neither of the two corresponds to the experience of adult foods such as wine, coffee, chili peppers, and all the possible variations of elaborate sour or bitter dishes stemming from intentions and projects other than "reawakening" the taste of childhood.

The notion of wisdom I utilize here—as usual, in a very pragmatic and basic sense—stems from the methodological attention paid to the phenomenological variety of food perceptions. It practically corresponds to a *syntonized*, sensitive, and skillful perception, able to recognize these differences, embedding them into a fulfilled experience. In other words, the wisdom of taste is a wise attitude that allows us to cross the three modes of access to the experience of food and their contamination. *Wisdom* is a noble word of great extension, which does not only refer to the tradition of Eastern thought, but also to the very birth of Western philosophy. As is well known, the ancient Greek schools characterized philosophy in terms of daily exercise, a theoretical practice aimed at a peaceful and happy life, thus connecting philosophy to ordinary experience and to behavioral patterns. In this context, a sage is someone who possesses a special type of wisdom that the Greeks called *phronesis*; it is through *phronesis* that a person is able to orient herself in different life situations and to choose what is most appropriate. The sage sets an example of virtuous behavior, which is propaedeutic to a balanced and fulfilling life. But why did I choose to use this word—*wisdom*—in an essay on the philosophy of food and the aesthetics of taste? The answer is just as surprising as it is trivial. The connection between taste and wisdom almost resides "in the things themselves" even if it has rarely been emphasized. The etymology of the word *wise*, or rather *sage*, has a double origin in Latin. According to one origin, it comes from *sapidus*, from the verb *sapio* (to know, to have taste); according to the other, it comes from *exagium* (in Greek *exagion*), from the verb *exigo* (to weigh, to examine, to assay, in the sense of trying and proving one's hand at something). An *essay*—in the sense of a text—therefore plays with wisdom in its twofold sense, always connected to the (mother) *tongue*: the essay is an attempt, an exploration, a test, an assay, a tasting. But the wise person is also the person who has the practical *wisdom* that allows him or her to move skillfully in accordance with the rhythm of experience.

In his inaugural lecture at the Collège de France in 1977, on the relationship between language and power, Roland Barthes—who also explored in the same years the concept of the neutral, which profoundly shaped his work—emphasized the limits of a pure theoretical conception of language and knowledge. With respect to the etymology of *sapientia*, characterizing the sensitive origin of taste, he made the following statement, which became famous: "No power, a bit of knowledge, a bit of wisdom, and as much *flavor* as possible." Barthes thus defines knowledge and wisdom as ethical-aesthetic attitudes starting from the awareness of the inseparable unity of sensory perceptions and the intelligible, of body and mind. In this light, wisdom does not correspond to pure cleverness and to logico-linguistic ability, but to an ecological and practical understanding of one's own psychophysical being where the primary and fundamental relationship with food is not denigrated. If the taste of wisdom is a flexible exploration of the environment through perceptual abilities that develop from the indissoluble bond between the mind and the senses, and if, among these encounters we have throughout the course of our life, the relationship with food stands out for its necessary importance, then we need a *wisdom of taste* as the flexible perception of food experiences. The gustatory experience can then promote this comprehensive attitude, which I propose to define as wisdom. What is, in fact, an experience? In German, there are two distinct terms for "experience," *Erfahrung* and *Erlebnis*.

The word *Erfahrung* refers to the idea of travel, because *fahren* in German means to travel. It defines a worldly and externalized experience, the encounter with the things of the world, "having" an experience and then becoming an expert, "acquiring" expertise. The word *Erlebnis*, on the other hand, is the lived and interior experience: "living" an experience, because *leben* in German means to live. Taste as an aesthetic relationship is as much an experience in the sense of *Erfahrung* as it is in the sense of *Erlebnis*. What we eat, in fact, contributes to "having an experience" while it is being accepted, internalized, and assimilated. Through a process of somatic assimilation, taste expertise promotes both an external and an internal transformation, so that we could also speak, as Richard Shusterman (2014) puts it, of a *somaesthetics of taste* relationship. Wisdom is the awareness of the many variables and processes in which these experiences occur, along with the ability to pass through them. The epigraph from Montaigne that opens this chapter is an example of gustatory wisdom: "If you make your pleasure depend on drinking good wine, you condemn yourself to the pain of sometimes drinking bad wine. We must have a *less exacting and freer* taste" (Montaigne 2002, bk. 2, chap. 2, p. 247, my emphasis). This sentence does not display an inadequate and careless attitude to food, or a superiority complex, but rather the opposite. It expresses extreme sensitivity for the differences and the variables that constitute the set of possible relationships, a sensitivity that wants to mold itself in accordance with things and that is the key to understanding the experience of taste.

In the history of aesthetics, of course, there have been positions that strongly emphasized the value of experience for forming a complete, active, practical, and wide-ranging aesthetic sensitivity, despite the predominant modern contemplative paradigm. I have repeatedly mentioned Dewey, but one also needs to call on the German poet, playwright, and philosopher Friedrich Schiller, author of a famous treatise *On the Aesthetic Education of Man* (1795), in which he proposed an aesthetic education that aims at having human beings develop their perceptive possibilities to the fullest, and at connecting aesthetics and art to social life and politics. However, the praise of experience on behalf of the aesthetics of taste must not be confused with a simple eulogy of vitalism, because the "lived" experience (*Erlebnis*) stems and develops from an encounter with external events (*Erfahrung*), which, in turn, set its limits. The experience of the different, the extraneous, and the exotic calls into question one's own critical and evaluative self-sufficiency, inviting exchange and negotiation. There is also another important aspect that prevents the leveling of the experience of food to vitalism, to the frenetic activity of gathering information and data that runs the risk of flattening the understanding of environment to the self-referential character of instantaneous emotion: the awareness of the relational, ecological, and biased character of our experiences. The wisdom of taste develops from that awareness.

WISE EXPERTISE (EPICURUS, HUME, AND DEWEY)

The dispute about the true meaning of Epicurus's thought and of Epicureanism is well known and very old. It began immediately after the philosopher's death and erupted precisely around the question of food. According to many interpreters, Epicurus did not profess any militancy for gastronomic delights; actually, since his writings even contain elements of disapproval of excesses and greed, he would serve as an example of a suspicious attitude toward perceptible enjoyment. One of the best-known readings in this direction is the one proposed by Karl Marx, who wrote his PhD dissertation on the different materialistic systems of Epicurus and Democritus. According to Marx, the philosophy of Epicurus does not derive—as the Stoic philosopher Chrysippus held—from the *Gastronomy* of the Sicilian poet Archestratus of Gela (in Greek, this lost book, cited by Athenaus, was also called *Hedypatheia*, "Life of Luxury"), but rather from the freedom of individual self-consciousness (Marx 2000). Marx's position is highly significant, because it expresses a materialistic thought that erases the vulgar and "low" enjoyment of food from its horizon. How can this interpretation be reconciled with the attribution to Epicurus of the aphorism given by Athenaeus in the *Deipnosophistae* already cited—"The origin and root of all good is the pleasure of the stomach; and all excessive efforts of wisdom have reference to the stomach"—which seems to promote a decidedly radical thought in favor of the gustatory pleasures? According to other authors (Symons 2007), and also in ordinary language, the adjective *Epicurean* is in fact an eponym of militancy in favor of the pleasure of conviviality and perceptible enjoyment. In the history of gastronomy, for example, in Escoffier and in Grimod de la Reynière, the name of Epicurus was associated with important dinners and refined culinary events.

I will now promote an interpretation of Epicurus (which is not strictly philological) as a key to encouraging gustatory wisdom following the proposal of a wise approach in the terms stated above. Let's take his most famous and popular piece of work, his "Letter to Menoeceus," where he summarizes his ethical doctrines. There are two passages where Epicurus explicitly refers to food. The first:

> The wise man does not deprecate life nor does he fear the cessation of life. The thought of life is no offence to him, nor is the cessation of life regarded as an evil. *And even as men choose of food not merely and simply the larger portion, but the more pleasant*, so the wise seek

to enjoy the time which is most pleasant and not merely that which is longest. (Epicurus 1925, 651–53, my emphasis)

The second:

Plain fare gives as much pleasure as a costly diet, . . . while bread and water confer the highest possible pleasure when they are brought to hungry lips. To habituate one's self, therefore, to simple and inexpensive diet supplies all that is needful for health, and enables a man to meet the necessary requirements of life without shrinking, and it places us in a better condition when we approach at intervals a costly fare and renders us fearless of fortune.

When we say, then, that pleasure is the end and aim, we do not mean the pleasures of the prodigal or the pleasures of sensuality, as we are understood to do by some through ignorance, prejudice, or wilful misrepresentation. By pleasure we mean the absence of pain in the body and of trouble in the soul. *It is not an unbroken succession of drinking-bouts and of revelry, not sexual love,* not the enjoyment of the fish and other delicacies of a luxurious table, which produce a pleasant life; it is sober reasoning, searching out the grounds of every choice and avoidance, and banishing those beliefs through which the greatest tumults take possession of the soul. (655–57, my emphasis)

The first passage says that the sage chooses foods based on their quality, not on their quantity. This attitude evidently considers the taste of foods and their intrinsic characteristics. But the second piece provides a necessary addition: simple flavors can give the *same pleasure* (*ísen edonèn*) as the most refined ones, which is to say that it is not the banquets in themselves and costly foods such as good fish that make a happy life. Attention to quality does not contradict the awareness of the ecology in which gustatory relationships happen. Epicurus professes neither the need for culinary refinement at all times, nor the denial of the pleasures of food, nor ideological austerity. For to claim that simple flavors *can* provide the same pleasure as the most refined ones, or that banquets and parties do not deliver happiness *in themselves*, without denying at the same time the chance to experience delicious and sumptuous cooking, means to express neither absolute preferences nor a priori hierarchies. It means putting perception back into its environment, that is, having the ability to retain changes of experience. Right afterward, in fact, the philosopher goes on to say that "the origin (*arché*) and maximum good (*mèghiston agathòv*) of all these things" are that practical ability, that knowing how to live and how to behave that the Greeks identified with wisdom, as expressed in the concept of *phronesis*.

It is then possible to translate *phronesis* into the concrete articulations of a specific taste expertise, according to the aforementioned indications given by philosophers like Hume and Dewey in describing the role of the critic and expert. Far from adopting a rigid and exclusive attitude, the expert was the one who proved able to interpret and understand different situations. Hume stressed the need for *common sense* and Dewey, in turn, insisted on the ability of connecting gustatory perception to its source, the food eaten, its characteristics and production methods. Epicurus, as well as Montaigne, added sensitivity to the different contexts in which the relationship with food takes place. Let me say explicitly that I do not take the wisdom of taste to be identical with expertise. Wisdom is a transversal attitude, which also contemplates the other modes of dealing with food, pleasure, and indifference. Nonetheless, a wise approach can be modulated in the specific articulations of dressed taste, hence also in expertise, and in the cultivation of gastronomy as an art of living. Here is a brief summary of four areas of potentiality of taste as expertise, as cultivated endocorporeal knowledge, starting with the wise approach to the experience of food.

— Wise taste capacity is the instrument with which to implement one's own "art of living": a practice of the self, an active care of the self (Foucault, 1990, 1992). This practice is an exercise that can discipline and transform the body, just like sport, thus increasing multisensory awareness. In fact, the relationship with food has immediate physical (weight, size, shape, and well-being) and mental (inebriation, joy, and fulfillment) effects and contributes to the reflection upon the relationship between moderation and excess.

— Wise taste capacity implements perceptual sensitivity toward little variations and nuances: minimal differences in qualitative characteristics of the objects enjoyed, but above all, minimal differences in the contexts of experience and the connections in which the qualities of the objects emerge. In this respect, taste expertise brings into play different degrees of ability in relation to different goals and objectives. These different devices that are activated in specific situations are the flexibility of taste expertise.

— Wise taste capacity is not acquiescent to extant cultural codes, but expresses critical potential. It promotes the ability to make independent choices and resist imposed models. In his work "Answering the Question: What Is Enlightenment?" Immanuel Kant described what he calls "emergence from . . . immaturity," and among other things he also mentioned food. He stated that one should not passively eat what others tell us to eat, *even if* they are doctors and nutritionists. The final judge is one's self, seen as the unity of mind and body: confidence in our senses must guide our food choices. As was already stated by the Salernitan School of Medicine, every single man should be his own best doctor. Moreover, one must always use personal proclivities as a filter in the framework of negotiation and interaction. Taste lives in the intersubjective dimension, and here, besides sharing, tensions and disagreements are possible.

— Wise taste capacity allows for exploring the connection between consumption and production in the food chain. It therefore allows a critical look at production issues, the environment, nature, and the economy. The aesthetics of taste as a relationship has to do with all this because it develops from an evolutionary and ecological vision, where the relationships between different perceptions are constructed via the ability to perceive new associations of meaning.

Regulation Without Rules

I warned that gustatory wisdom is a general attitude that covers a larger area than wise expertise. Thus, there is more to the wisdom of taste than "being an expert." This wisdom requires an awareness of the procedural and contextual nature of the experience of food, and it is structured along *bifocal* lines: from very far away and from up close, in a complementary, integrated, or alternating fashion. Looking at food from up close, in fact, runs the risk of neglecting or denying the ecological and relational dimension inherent in it; on the other hand, standing too far back risks misreading its essential value. This complex mode is not molded as a *dominant* approach to the food experience. There is more than dominion, because there is more than just visual perception and assimilating incorporation. Wisdom is the ability to move between tension and relaxation, between activating and deactivating deliberate attention toward the food tasted, in a consideration that sways between the maximum and the minimum of the importance accorded to it. To strive for wisdom, one must be able to go beyond the domain of mere vision and mere incorporation and experiment with multidimensional and multisensory approaches.

Starting from Chinese aesthetics, François Jullien defends an enriching perspective on wisdom, and allows us to take new roads by introducing thriving connections (Jullien 1995, 2004). Perhaps no other civilization has developed an attention to food and cooking similar to the Chinese: a huge variety of food items and recipes, together with a rich, nonspecialist, everyday vocabulary and the existence of public places for eating already during Marco Polo's time, speak of the high regard in which eating and taste were held. In ancient China, being educated also meant having the ability to appreciate food and to express that appreciation in the appropriate linguistic manner (Anderson 1988; Yu-Fu Tuan 2005). It is therefore only logical to take a brief look at this seemingly remote conceptual universe in which the value of food is a known and shared paradigm. Rather than speaking of irreducible differences in this case, it would be more appropriate to speak of prospects that are unexplored and marginalized, yet present in "our" universe. According to Jullien, the main characteristic of the Chinese sage is not personifying any idea or having exclusive inclinations or rigid preferences. Wisdom is a *transitional thought* between different, even extreme or opposite positions in the *continuum* of experience. *Transitional thought* is not a thought of rule, but of *regulation*: as one tunes a musical instrument, the sage tunes his perceptions and his actions to the flow of experience. For our purposes, this ability, at the same time mental and practical, rational and sensitive, has much in common with the notion of *phronesis*. The sage has *phronesis* and knows how to pass from one extreme to the other. The flexibility of his perception does not regard "the golden mean," that median position in static equilibrium between opposite poles, but the ability to move, fluctuate, or drift lightly. With respect to the relationship with food, the sage will therefore know when to enjoy, to recognize, or even to remain indifferent according to the occasions.

The reasoning above also provides us with an argument for limiting the definition of taste as "pleasure that knows and knowledge that enjoys" given by Giorgio Agamben, which has cropped up more than once in this essay. It is a limit that the cases of pleasure, as the relaxation of knowledge and of indifference, as retraction from attention, have already foreshadowed since these gustatory encounters did not seem to lean completely on the side of "constructive" subjectivity. Instead, Agamben's definition seems to suggest such a view, which ties the polarities of pleasure and knowledge always together without giving their disarticulation, in certain contexts, even the slightest chance. But the experience of food is not necessarily only an experience of *construction*, but also one of *hospitality*. One can have an experience even just through pleasure or knowledge; one can have naked, instantaneous pleasure as well as a purely intellectual pleasure for the food tasted. Taste can therefore be inflected as a pleasure when one enjoys, as knowledge when one knows, and as indifferent neutrality when the taste relationship withdraws, because something more meaningful emerges during the experience. Gustatory wisdom is the awareness of this process along with the skillful ability to regulate it on the grounds of the concrete relationships with the objects in the environment around us. More importantly, this does not mean controlling and managing everything, but rather perceiving when and how it is appropriate and convenient *to lose* control. Living a taste experience means *being inside* a universe of relations for the time required, and then leaving it to develop new connections and build new relationships in another gustatory scene. Eating bread or fruit, considering one's equilibrium and weight, limiting oneself; exaggerating, not paying attention to getting fat, getting drunk, or feasting: these different and even opposite experiences can all find aesthetic legitimacy, as long as they are accompanied by awareness and by the capacity to harmonize the inside and the outside, the perception and the percept.

Gustatory wisdom, however, is not a programmatically passive or accommodating attitude. Its guideline is: *it depends.* Complying with dominant codes and values would in fact mean betraying the profound meaning of the relationship with food—openness, respect, enjoyment, improvement, criticism, and resistance. Gustatory wisdom fights codices when it is *appropriate* to fight them, when the conditions of experience require it. If, for example, in a restaurant you were served fish that was supposed to be freshly caught, and if that was *not* the case and you were sure of this because of your expertise or owing to other information you might have, then you would have every right to protest. This would be a wise and legitimate attitude in response to dishonesty and deceit. Who should be held responsible though? Perhaps not the waiter, who might be unaware of the problem. And what if the cook, too, were ignorant of the matter? Of course, ignorance is not allowed for the cook, but she may have been tricked by the fisherman. Situations may be complex and require specific individual responses that can vary on occasion. Wisdom is this critical vigilance. It is passion for the differences and patience; it is not self-referential and concedes very little to narcissism.

The wisdom of taste recognizes the importance of training, education, and expertise. Yet the reaction to something ugly or bad can be either complete refusal or comprehensive acceptance, produced by different elements: compassionate, comic, social, or emotional ones. A bad meal offered by someone who believes to be offering a good one, an indigestible sandwich eaten on a holiday trip in a bar run by uncaring people: the meal remains bad, the sandwich remains indigestible, but even such experiences can be part of a broader picture that redeems and transforms them into opportunities for pleasure. Wisdom does not like snobbery, except when it is ascribable to a specific strategy of (dis)armed resistance.

FLEXIBILITY: THE FOREST AND THE COAST

There is an Italian proverb that well expresses the skillful ability to transition, know-how as adaptability and flexibility: *to belong to the forest and to the coast*. Forest and coast are polar opposites in imagery and lifestyles: the cold, the shade, the frugality, and the wildness of the woods contrast with the heat, sun, riches, and sophistication of the coast. This motto has a general application and can be applied to eating: the food of the forest and sea food are different—berries, foraged plants, roots, and game on the one hand; fish, farmed fruits, and vegetables on the other. In the ancient world, forest and sea also represented the respective polarities of nature and culture. Following the advice of the Chinese sage, as well as of Epicurus and Montaigne, *belonging to the forest and to the coast* thus means giving up any rigid leaning of the self, developing a malleability that makes it possible to go through different gustatory experiences: the high and the low, pleasure and knowledge, attention and indifference, nature and culture, wild and refined.

In his reflections, Jullien emphasized this attitude with the phrase *ça va*, "it's ok" or "it's going well"—and the motto *to belong to the forest and to the coast* precisely translates this attitude. If you are *invited* to a party, you will drink what there is; if you go to a *friend's* house, you will eat what is offered. These two elementary cases of daily life are especially significant, because hospitality and friendship are relational activities frequently involving food, thanks to which enjoyment and pleasure are not necessarily bound only to olfactory and flavor appreciation, but also to motivations partly extrinsic to the quality of the food. If we were offered a mediocre meal by a friend, not for a deliberate reason but out of unawareness or a lack of means, we would not be allowed to reject it. *Phronesis* would guide us toward a feeling of appreciation based on the recognition and understanding of the overall relationship: a gift is not to be rejected. "Guest" is an ambivalent notion. Usually we refer to the *active* relationship when we emphasize the value of hospitality: the value of accommodating someone. In the eighth book of the *Metamorphoses*, Ovid tells the myth of Philemon and Baucis. The gods Jupiter and Mercury, being in the region of Phrygia in human form, were visiting some villages, asking for hospitality. Nobody let them in with the one exception of an elderly couple who lived in a small and pitiful hut, made of reeds and mud. Philemon and Baucis immediately prepared a modest meal (of cabbage and pork shoulder) and a bed for their tired guests. According to the myth, Jupiter afterward unleashed his fury against the Phrygians and destroyed all the villages, saving only Philemon and Baucis, and transformed their home into a beautiful temple. But the apology of hospitality and conviviality told by this myth needs to be thought all the way through also in the other direction: the value of *being accommodated*. The ethics of accommodating coincides with the ethics of being a guest. Moreover, the Latin word for "guest" is *hospes* (hence, *hospital*), which also means "host," that is, *the one who sustains a stranger*, who receives him and cooks for him. Hospitality is therefore conviviality, and conviviality is the acceptance *of* the *hospes*, in the double meaning of the genitive: accepting a guest, inviting her, as well as the guest who accepts what she receives (Perullo 2011). Wisdom pertains to the awareness of hospitality. Wisdom is a hospitable vocation.

Of course, there are other possibilities. A case that invokes a different attitude regards the relationship in which taste does not agree with the gift, where instead it is the instrument for measuring an exchange, the judge of an economic performance. When we pay a lot for eating and drinking, carefully choosing the food we would like to cook, or select a promising gourmet restaurant, our gustatory compass becomes active. It turns into expertise and it sparks the relative critical high points, directing itself mainly toward (analytically or synthetically) assessing the *qualitative* elements that motivate its measurement in money. Food in its "intrinsic" value, and its ethical and symbolic values, is translated, via gusto, into the great universal quantifier, viewable in a price tag. This fact, which is so common in our lives, should not suggest that wisdom is a luxury. Even when food seems reduced to a mere commodity, it is possible to develop more complex enhancement strategies related to nonmeasurable qualities, which once again go back to the *embodiment* of taste as aesthetic relationship.

To belong to the forest and to the coast does not mean failing to recognize and perceive the bad and the ugly: it means understanding them in a wider framework, which also includes the possibility of recovering them (without necessarily justifying it) at a different level. Too rigid preferences and excessively acute leanings risk turning into hang-ups, cages that one is unable to leave and that preclude the possibility of enjoying unpredictable experiences. Above all, however, they do not capture the characteristic, relational, and flexible dynamics of taste, imposing the construction of ex post theoretical models to fictitiously justify the professed preference. A look at professional food criticism shows that this approach is widespread: perfectly legitimate but negotiated, historical, and procedural value expressions are "rationally" theorized—of course, until the next season, when a new paradigm will certainly challenge one or the other. From this point of view, wine is again a perfect example: changes in the aesthetic properties of the vocabulary of wine tasting in the last twenty years—for example, the transition from "structure" to "drinkability," from "density" to "lightness" as descriptive values—are there for everyone to see (Perullo 2012a). However, wisdom does not exhort the *absolute* renunciation of one's own inclinations either; it rather makes one aware of their easing up through the watchful exercise of *the corner of one's eye*. These inclinations precisely express special and partial relationships, never complete and final ones, so it is advisable always to practice an alien perspective—in the sense not only of *other* tastes, of foods and beverages from other cultures, but also of our *internal* othernesses. Looking out of the corner of our eye will make us reflect on and draw consequences from circumstances such as the fact that years ago I liked completely different food from today; and anyway, I don't always need great wines—I also drink simple wines just for the pleasure of it and often I feel like having water or wine, but without thinking about it, or even beer, which is perfect when I'm having a good time and anything is fine with me, when I'm with the one(s) I love. (Proust: "But while I was at the Swann's I would have been unable to say whether or not it was really tea I was drinking. And even if I had known, I would have gone on drinking it.")

I argued that hospitality has to do with giving and accepting in both directions. However, the *hospes*—the host or the guest—is not only the foreign *friend*; he can also prove to be *hostile*, the enemy. Whoever hosts must contemplate the possibility of conflict and discord. Conviviality—from *cum vivere*, "to live together"—is the emblematic, physical, and metaphorical space of the twofold possibility inherent in the experience of food. Sharing and discord generally characterize the social essence of human life, and eating together is one of its most radical and distinctive features. Conviviality can therefore represent a gym for refining the wisdom of taste. But of course, it needs to be open, "hospitable," and not rigid. From this point of view, if the gastronomic brotherhoods always risk being self-referential and closed, *open conviviality* is a bastion of resistance against the consequences of the attitudes of complacency and *social distinction* (Bourdieu 1984) and *conspicuous consumption* (Veblen 1899). The gourmand, the compulsive, and the indifferent eater can find elements for reflection with respect to their hardened ways in open conviviality, which puts them back into the game with new perspectives on confronting others. Conviviality fosters the ability to listen and the willingness to do so; wisdom models itself on this attitude, which is the opposite of the assertive approach of seeking immediate consensus.

Conviviality was thought to be important from the beginning of philosophy, even by thinkers like Plato, who did not devote any positive philosophical attention to the sense of taste. But Epicurus, in another aphorism attributed to him, states that before you eat or drink anything, carefully consider with whom you eat or drink rather than what you eat or drink (Epicurus 1925). The sage's taste therefore is aimed not exclusively at food objects, but also at contexts: on appropriate occasions, any food will do at any level. Unrestrained drunkenness or the most frugal meal can become meaningful in an appropriate convivial situation, and for an advanced sensitivity, even loneliness can become a convivial experience sui generis, that is, an interesting and rewarding relationship with food and drink for someone seeking a solitary meal (at home or in a restaurant) or drink under certain circumstances. The ability to listen and understand the other, typical of wise behavior, is expressed in the attitude that recognizes the limits of one's inclinations and preferences, starting from that which according to Montaigne is the most important social virtue: *empathy*. The wisdom of taste can also be understood as the constant exercise in gustatory empathy in situations of diversity and contention. In other words, the sage's taste empathy is a "reversed" empathy. It consists in understanding—and feeling—why a food we fail to appreciate is popular, or why a drink that leaves us indifferent or worse is so well liked: this ability is the height of the wisdom of taste.

"Everyday diplomacy" is what the sociologist Richard Sennett called the strategy used in dealing with people we do not understand and to whom we have difficulties relating, a strategy used for the superior purpose of the "common good" and for the *joint* creation of something positive (Sennett 2012). We can in the same manner interpret the wisdom of taste as a flexible device—being able to pass between tension and relaxation, the activating and deactivating of deliberate attention toward the tasted food—as the daily diplomacy of convivial relations. The relationship with food, in fact, is almost always mediated by the relationship with others: diners and consumers, but also other *preparers* and processors of food. The space of conviviality is not exclusively defined by the relationship between tasters; those who prepare the food must also be taken into account. The differences in cooking styles express complex social and historical facts, and (amateur and professional) chefs themselves go through changes in their taste and their relationship with the raw materials in the course of their lives. This finding further enhances the overall situation, but also undermines any assertive judgment and gives new impetus to the dialogical character of convivial experience.

TAKE MY ADVICE

The wisdom of taste suggests an attitude, it "advises" certain behavior and, true to its nature, does not produce strict enunciations. At the end of this essay, it might therefore be useful to outline what has been gained on a theoretical level and summarize it in a final list of practical information according to the model of *phronesis*—knowledge that is both *know-how* and knowing how to relate to the "world." These guidelines follow directly from the domain we have discussed, that of taste as an aesthetic relationship and as experience, but they are so general that they can be applied to other kinds of "everyday diplomacy" with the environment and people. The indications, however (and this is my last specification), are just a road map: not precepts, and definitely not dogma. Please take them as gentle suggestions.

— Only talk about the things you know or experiences you have actually had: the food and drink you have actually eaten, the cuisines you have tried. Do not indulge in compulsive chatter and superficial assertions. Do not be quick with an opinion. It is not always necessary to have one or to make judgments. Take time to think things over long and hard, and if you have doubts, keep them until they dissolve on their own. And if they don't dissolve, learn to live with them. However, if you would like to become an "expert," strengthen your ability to have gustatory empathy before making "negative" and derogatory judgments, and look for all the extenuating circumstances in someone else's choices. Weigh your words well: they are always important. Don't fall back on "hearsay."

— When approaching a planned aesthetic experience, lower your horizons of expectation, practice detachment and relaxation. An aesthetic experience is not a competition between the users and the makers. Drinking a special bottle of wine or eating dishes prepared by a famous chef are not actions that lead to hand-to-hand combat with these objects and their creators, but actions that try to effect agreement, making it possible to enjoy them in the best possible manner. The aesthetic experience arises from a successful relationship, from an achieved negotiation. To succeed, a relationship requires availability and openness. Nothing is more wrong, therefore, than approaching a situation with preventive suspicion, or with the idea that one is about to be tricked. In the case of repeat experiences, try forgetting the prior ones, if possible. This is not to call for a cancelation of critical sense; on the contrary, critical sense (in Greek *krinein* means to distinguish, to weigh) arises when perception is extended and includes, not when it wears thin and smugly endorses established patterns and comfortable codes.

— Keep a balance between tension and relaxation, between attention and disinterest. Develop massive doses of irony and self-irony. Irony is the key to wisdom: do not take yourself too seriously, but live the present experience to its fullest and believe in what you do. Be passionate and ironic, and therefore also autoironic. This twofold state is difficult to achieve, but very rewarding and functional; it pertains to both the mind and the body. Consequently, don't fret about the details. First, try to feel the whole and then maybe the details, not the other way around. The experience of food is a complex and synthetic experience, not a discrete and analytical one that comes later and for specific purposes.

— Be passionate and not just emotional; cultivate passion. Integrate reminiscences with memory, and practice it. Passion lasts longer, rises vertically, recalls buried blazes of memory and traces of childhood. Emotion is fleeting and flows evenly: it "surfs," as one would say today. It mainly stirs memories, it is typical of adolescents and adults, and it expresses the illusory belief that one can buy everything, as in a supermarket. Obviously, there is nothing wrong with immediate emotions and memories, but food also requires depth, pauses, repetitions, lengths of time, whereby rich identities and close relations develop. So, dear gastronomes, do not exaggerate with photos and videos: you risk really not perceiving the food and drink that you have before you, and that is waiting to be received by you. Allow the experience to pass through your attention into memory, which will select what is really important.

— Do not have absolute preferences and inclinations. It is preferable to think that the best wine or the best dish is the last one you had, or the one you will enjoy the next day. And this is not in contrast with the praise of the aforementioned passion: a passion for food *is not* fetishism for its objects, for food and drink. The passion for food is a *passion for the experience of food* as a passion for life and living itself, for the pleasure of the relationship and the conflict of incorporation.

Eating and drinking are the most common and exemplary actions of our relationship with the outside—with what we receive, assimilate, and understand, which nonetheless remains *other* than us and which, as such, must be respected. So, lithely pass from top to bottom with pleasure, from the most polished and sophisticated to the involuntarily vulgar. But scorn arrogant and deliberate presumptuousness and vulgarity. That is all.

NOTES

INTRODUCTION

1. [Note for the English translation: I play with certain subtleties of the Italian language. In Italian, the verb *to taste* can also be reflexive, reflecting the experience back onto the subject. Hence "taste is tasted." In addition, the verb's etymology is related to *saggio*, "a written essay," intended as a direct exploration of a subject. Understanding taste in its content of experience signifies understanding it in its *radical sense*, including its complex and procedural factors.]

SECOND MODE OF ACCESS: KNOWLEDGE

1. [Note for the English translation: The epigraph is missing from the English translation.]

REFERENCES

Agamben, G. 2015. *Gusto*. Macerata: Quodlibet.

Allhoff, F., and D. Monroe, eds. 2007. *Food and Philosophy: Eat, Think, and Be Merry*. Oxford: Blackwell.

Anderson, E. N. 1988. *The Food of China*. New Haven: Yale University Press.

Assouly, O. 2008. *Le capitalisme esthètique: Essai sur l'industrialisation du goût*. Paris: Cerf.

Athenaeus of Naukratis. 1929. *The Deipnosophists, Or, Banquet of the Learned*. Loeb Classical Library. Cambridge, Mass.: Harvard University Press.

Auvrey, C., and D. Spence. 2007. "The Multisensory Perception of Flavor." *Consciousness and Cognition* 17:1016–31.

Barbery, M. 2009. *Gourmet Rhapsody*. New York: Europa Editions.

Barthes, R. 1997. "Toward a Psychosociology of Contemporary Food Consumption." In *Food and Culture: A Reader*, edited by C. Counihan and P. Van Esterik, 20–27. New York: Routledge. Originally published in 1961.

Baugè, B. 2012. "On the Idea of Novelty in Cuisine: A Brief Historical Insight." *International Journal of Gastronomy and Food Science*: 5–14.

Beauchamp, G. K., and L. Bartoshuk, eds. 1997. *Tasting and Smelling*. San Diego: Academic Press.

Benjamin, W. 2008. *The Work of Art in the Age of Mechanical Reproduction*. London: Penguin.

Berry, W. 1990. "The Pleasures of Eating." In *What Are People For?* New York: Farrar, Straus and Giroux.

Borghini, A. 2014 "Authenticity in Food." In *Encyclopedia of Food and Agricultural Ethics*, edited by P. B. Thomson and D. M. Kaplan. Dordrecht: Springer.

Bourdieu, P. 1984. *The Distinction: A Social Critic of the Judgement of Taste*. Cambridge, Mass.: Harvard University Press.

Boutaud, J. J. 2005. *Le sens gourmand*. Paris: Jean-Paul Rocher.

Brillat-Savarin, A. 2009. *The Physiology of Taste or Meditations on Transcendental Gastronomy*. Translated by M.F.K. Fisher. New York: Alfred A. Knopf. Originally published 1825.

Burnham, D., and O. M. Skilleås. 2012. "Patterns of Attention: 'Project' and the Phenomenology of Aesthetic Perception." *Wineworld: New Essays on Wine, Taste, Philosophy and Aesthetics: Rivista di Estetica* 51 (3): 117–36.

Calvino, I. 1977. *The Baron in the Trees*. Boston: Mariner.

——. 1984. "Theft in a Pastry Shop." In *Difficult Loves*. New York: Harcourt Brace Jovanovich. Originally published in 1949.

——. 1988. *Under the Jaguar Sun*. New York: Harcourt Brace Jovanovich. Originally published in 1986.

Casey, B. J., L. H. Somerville, I. H. Gotlib, O. Ayduk, N. T. Franklin, M. K. Askren, J. Jonides, M. G. Berman, N. L. Wilson, T. Teslovich, G. Glover, V. Zayas, W. Mischel, and Y. Shoda. 2011. "Behavioral and Neural Correlates of Delay of Gratification 40 Years Later." *Psychological and Cognitive Sciences*, August 29.

Chapman, H. A., D. A. Kin, J. M. Susskind, and A. K. Anderson. 2009. "In Bad Taste: Evidence for the Oral Origins of Moral Disgust." *Science* 323 (February 27): 1222–26.

Chiva, M. 1985. *Le doux et l'amer: Sensation gustative, Emotion e communication chez le jeune enfant*. Paris: Presses universitaires de France.

Coccia, E. 2011. *La vita sensibile*. Bologna: Il Mulino.

Cooper, A. 1998. *A Woman's Place Is in the Kitchen*. New York: Van Nostrand Reinhold.

Counihan, C., and P. Van Esterik, eds. 1997. *Food and Culture: A Reader*. Oxford: Routledge.

Curtin, D., and L. M. Heldke, eds. 1992. *Cooking, Eating, Thinking. Transformative Philosophies of Food*. Bloomington: Indiana University Press.

Darwin, C. 1965. *The Expressions of the Emotions in Man and Animals*. Chicago: University of Chicago Press.

DeLillo, D. 2001. *The Body Artist*. New York: Scribner.

Derrida, J. 1981. "Economimesis." *Diacritics* 11 (2): 2–25.

——. 1992. "'Il faut bien manger' ou le calcul du sujet." In *Points de suspension*. Paris: Galilée.

Dewey, J. 1980. *Art as Experience*. In *The Collected Works of John Dewey: The Later Works, 1925–1953*, vol. 10. New York: Perigee. Originally published in 1935.

Dissanayake, E. 2000. *Art and Intimacy: How the Arts Began*. Seattle: University of Washington Press.

Dubos, J. B. 1748. *Critical Reflections on Poetry, Painting and Music*. Originally published in 1719. 3 vols. Translated by T. Nugent. London: J. Nourse.

Eaton Muelder, M. 1997. "Aesthetics: The Mother of Ethics?" In *Journal of Aesthetics and Art Criticism* 55 (4): 355–64.

Epicurus. 1925. "Letter to Menoeceus." In *Lives of Eminent Philosophers*, vol. 2, by Diogenes Laertius, translated by R. D. Hicks. Cambridge, Mass.: Harvard University Press.

Flandrin, J. L., and M. Montanari, eds. 1999. "From Dietetics to Gastronomy: The Liberation of the Gourmet." In *Food: A Culinary History*, 418–32. New York: Columbia University Press.

Foster Fraser, J. 1989. *Round the World on a Wheel*. London: Futura. Originally published in 1899.

Foucault, M. 1990. *The History of Sexuality*. Vol. 3, *The Care of Self*. London: Penguin. Originally published in 1984.

——. 1992. *The History of Sexuality*. Vol. 2, *The Use of Pleasure*. London: Penguin.

Fourier, C. 1996. *Fourier: The Theory of the Four Movements*. Edited by Gareth Stedman Jones and Ian Patterson. Cambridge Texts in the History of Political Thought. Cambridge: Cambridge University Press. Originally published in 1808.

Gibson, J. J. 1966. *The Senses Considered as Perceptual Systems*. New York: Cornell University Press.

Glanz, K., M. Basil, E. Maibach, J. Goldberg, and D. Snyder. 1998. "Why Americans Eat What They Do: Taste, Nutrition, Cost, Convenience, and Weight Control Concerns as Influences on Food Consumption." *Journal of the American Dietetic Association* 98 (10): 1118–26.

Goldstein, D. 2010. "Lévinas and the Ontology of Eating." *Gastronomica: The Journal of Food and Culture* 10 (3): 34–44.

Hadot, P. 1995. *Philosophy as a Way of Life*. Edited by A. Davidson. Malden, Mass.: Blackwell.

Halpern, G. M. 2005. *The Case for Pleasure*. Typescript donated by the author.

Hamilton, R., and V. Todolì, eds. 2009. *Food for Thought/Thought for Food*. New York: Actar.

Harris, M. 2006. *Buono da mangiare*. Torino: Einaudi. Originally published in 1985.

Hegel, G.W.F. 1975. *Aesthetics. Lecture on Fine Art*. Translated by T. M. Knox. Oxford: Clarendon. Originally published in 1842.

Heidegger, M. 2002. "The Age of the World Picture." In *Off the Beaten Track*. Cambridge: Cambridge University Press. Originally published in 1938.

Hillman, J. 2006. "Politics of Beauty." In *City and Soul: Uniform Edition, vol. 2*, edited by R. J. Leaver. Washington, D.C.: Spring.

Holley, A. 2006. *Le cerveau gourmand*. Paris: Odile Jacob.

Hume, D. 1909–14. "Of the Standard of Taste." In *English Essays: Sidney to Macaulay*. New York: P. F. Collier and Son.

Iggers, J. 2007. "Who Needs a Critic? The Standard of Taste and the Power of Branding." In Allhoff and Monroe, *Food and Philosophy*, 88–101.

Ingold, T. 2000. *The Perception of the Environment*. London: Routledge.

——. 2013. *Making*. London: Routledge.

Irigaray, L. 1985. *To Speak Is Never Neutral*. Ithaca: Cornell University Press.

Jullien, F. 1995. *The Propensity of Things: Toward a History of Efficacy in China*. New York: Zone.

——. 2004. *Treatise on Efficacy: Between Western and Chinese Thinking*. Honolulu: University of Hawaii Press.

——. 2007. *In Praise of Blandness: Proceeding from Chinese Thought and Aesthetics*. New York: Zone.

Kant, I. 1999. *Critique of Pure Reason*. Edited by P. Guyer and A. W. Wood. Cambridge: Cambridge University Press. Originally published in 1790.

Kaplan, D. ed. 2012. *The Philosophy of Food*. Berkeley: University of California Press.

Kass, L. R. 1999. *The Hungry Soul: Eating and the Perfecting of Our Nature*. New York: Free Press.

Korsmeyer, C. 1999. *Making Sense of Taste*. Ithaca: Cornell University Press.

——. 2004. *Gender and Aesthetics: An Introduction*. London: Routledge.

——, ed. 2005. *The Taste Culture Reader: Experiencing Food and Drink*. Oxford: Berg.

Korthals, M. 2008, "The Birth of Philosophy and Contempt for Food." *Gastronomica* 8 (3): 62–69.

Kuhen, G. 2012. "Tasting the World: Environmental Aesthetics and Food as Art." *Contemporary Pragmatism* 9 (1): 85–98.

Le Breton, D. 2006. *La saveur du monde:Une anthropologie des sens* . Prais: Metalie.

Lemke, H. 2008. *The Ethics of Taste: Principles of a Philosophy of Food or a New Gastrosophy*. www.haraldlemke.de.

Leroi-Gourhan, A. 1964–65. *Le geste et la parole*. 2 vols. Paris: Albin Michel.

Lévinas, E. 1988. *Existence and Existents*. Dordrecht: Kluwer.

Levinson, J. 2005. *Aesthetics Concepts*. In *Oxford Companion to Philosophy*, new ed. Oxford: Oxford University Press.

Martinelli, D. 2010. *A Critical Companion to Zoosemiotics: People, Paths, Ideas*. Dordrecht: Springer.

Marx, K. 2000. "The Difference Between the Democritean and Epicurean Philosophy of Nature" (1841). In *Selected Writings*, edited by D. McLean. Oxford: Oxford University Press.

Mauss, M. 1934. "Les Techniques du corps." *Journal de Psychologie* 32:3–4.

Mennella, J. A., C. P. Jagnow, and G. K. Beauchamp. 2001. "Prenatal and Postanatal Flavor Learning by Human Infants." *Pediatrics* 6 (107).

Monroe D. 2007. "Can Food Be Art? The Problem of Consumption." In Allhoff and Monroe, *Food and Philosophy*.

Montaigne, M. 2002. *The Complete Essays of Montaigne*. Stanford: Stanford University Press. Originally published in 1588.

Montanari, M. 1998. *La faim et l'abondance: Histoire de l'alimentation en Europe*. Paris: Seuil.

——. 2006. *Food Is Culture*. New York: Columbia University Press.

Mulder Eaton, M. 1997. "Aesthetics: The Mother of Ethics?" *Journal of Aesthetics and Art Criticism* 55 (4): 355–64.

Noble, A. C. 2006. "Describing the Indescribable." *Food Science and Technology International* 20 (3): 32–35.

Nothomb, A. 1996. *The Stranger Next Door*. New York: Henry Holt.

——. 2003. *The Character of Rain*. New York: St. Martin's Press.

——. 2006. *The Life of Hunger*. London: Faber and Faber.

Onfray, M. 1990. *Le ventre des philosophes: Critique de la raison diététique*. Paris: Les Livres de Poche Biblio.

Palahniuk, C. 2002. *Lullaby*. New York: Anchor.

Parasecoli, F. 2005. "Feeding Hard Bodies: Food and Masculinities in Men's Fitness Magazines." *Food and Foodways* 13:17–37.

Perniola, M. 1991. *Del sentire*. Torino: Einaudi.

Perullo, N. 2006. *Per un'estetica del cibo*. Palermo: Aesthetica Preprint.

——. 2008. *L'altro gusto. Saggi di estetica gastronomica*. Pisa: ETS.

——. 2010. *Filosofia della gastronomia laica*. Roma: Meltemi.

——. 2011a. *La scena del senso: A partire da Wittgenstein e Derrida*. Pisa: ETS.

——. 2011b. "Esperienza estetica, cucina, gastronomia." *Estetica: Studi e ricerche* 1.

——, ed. 2012a. *Wineworld: New Essays on Wine, Taste, Philosophy and Aesthetics: Rivista di Estetica* 51 (3).

——. 2012b. "Wineworld: Making, Tasting, Drinking, Being." In Perullo, *Wineworld*.

——. 2013. *La cucina è arte? Filosofia della passione culinaria*. Roma: Carocci.

——, ed. 2014. *Cibo, estetica e arte: Percorsi tra semiotica e storia*. Pisa: ETS.

Petrini, C. 2007. *Slow Food Nation: Why Our Food Should Be Good, Clean, and Fair*. New York: Random House.

Pollan, M. 2006. *The Omnivore's Dilemma*. New York: Penguin.

——. 2008. *In Defence of Food*. New York: Penguin.

Prescott, J. 2012. *Taste Matters: Why We Like the Foods We Do*. London: Reaktion.

Proust, M. 2003a. *In Search of Lost Time: In the Shadow of Young Girls in Flower*. London: Penguin. Originally published in 1919.

——. 2003b. *In Search of Lost Time: The Way by Swann's*. London: Penguin. Originally published in 1913.

Russell, B. 2004. "'Useless' Knowledge." In *In Praise of Idleness, and Other Essays*. New York: Routledge. Originally published in 1935.

Russo, L. ed. 2000. *Il Gusto: Storia di un'idea estetica*. Palermo: Aesthetica.

Saito, Y. 2007 *Everyday Aesthetics*. Oxford: Oxford University Press.

Scabin, D. 2008. "Ecco la mia morale del gusto." Interview by Francesca Angeleri. *Luxury24*. www.luxury24.ilsole24ore.com/GustoMete/2008/02/davide-scabin-chef_1.php.

Schiller, F.1967. *On the Aesthetic Education of Man*. Translated by E. M. Wilkinson and L. A. Willoughby. Oxford: Oxford University Press. Originally published in 1794.

Schivelbusch, W. 1992. *Tastes of Paradise: A Social History of Spices, Stimulants, and Intoxicants*. New York: Pantheon.

Scruton, R. 2010. *I Drink Therefore I Am: A Philosopher's Guide to Wine*. London: Bloomsbury Academic.

Sennett, R. 2009. *The Craftsman*. London: Penguin.

——. 2012. *Together: The Rituals, Pleasures and Politics of Cooperation*. New Haven: Yale University Press.

Serres, M. 2008. *The Five Senses: A Philosophy of Mingled Bodies*. New York: Continuum.

Shapin, S. 1998. "The Philosopher and the Chicken." In *Science Incarnate: Historical Embodiments of Natural Knowledge*, edited by C. Lawrence and S. Shapin, 21–50. Chicago: University of Chicago Press.

——. 2007. "Expertise, Common Sense and the Atkins Diet." In *Public Science in Liberal Democracy*, edited by J. M. Porter and P. W. Phillips. Toronto: Toronto University Press.

——. 2011. *Changing Tastes: How Things Tasted in the Early Modern Period and How They Taste Now.* Uppsala: Uppsala Universitet.

——. 2012. "The Sciences of Subjectivity." In *Social Studies of Sciences* 42 (2): 170–184.

Shusterman, R. 1992. *Pragmatist Aesthetics: Living Beauty, Rethinking Art.* Cambridge, Mass.: Blackwell.

——. 2014. "Somaesthetics and Gastronomy: Reflections on the Art of Eating." Published in Italian translation in *Cibo, estetica e arte: Percorsi tra semiotica e storia*, edited by N. Perullo. Pisa: ETS.

Sibley, F. 2007. *Approach to Aesthetics.* Edited by J. Benson, B. Redfern, and J. Roxbee Cox. Oxford: Oxford University Press.

Smith, B., ed. 2007. *Questions of Taste: Wine and Philosophy.* Oxford: Signal.

Symons, M. 2007. "Epicurus, the Foodies' Philosopher." In Allhoff and Monroe, *Food and Philosophy.*

"Summa de saporibus, testo anonimo del XIII secolo." 1991. In "The Superiority of Taste," edited by C. Burnett, special issue, *Journal of the Warburg and Courtauld Institutes.*

Tatarkiewicz, W. 1980. *History of Six Ideas: An Essay in Aesthetics.* Berlin: Springer.

Taylor, A. J., and D. D. Roberts, eds. 2004. *Flavor Perception.* Oxford: Blackwell.

Telfer, E. 1996. *Food for Thought.* London: Routledge.

Torday, P. 2008. *The Irresistible Inheritance of Wilberforce.* London: Phoenix.

Trubek, A. B. "Ethics of Gustatory Pleasure." In *Encyclopedia of Food and Agricultural Ethics*, edited by P. B. Thomson and D. M. Kaplan. Dordrecht: Springer.

Veblen, T. 1899. *The Theory of the Leisure Class: An Economic Study in the Evolution of Institutions.* New York: Macmillan.

Wittgenstein, L. 1998. *Culture and Value.* Edited by G. H. von Wright. London: Wiley-Blackwell.

——. 2009. *Philosophical Investigations.* London: Wiley-Blackwell. Originally published in 1953.

Yu-Fu Tuan. 2005. "Pleasures of the Proximate Senses." In Korsmeyer, *The Taste Culture Reader*, 226–34.

INDEX

Achatz, Grant, 39
addiction and compulsive behavior,
    78–80
Adrià, Ferran, 18–19, 20–21
adult flavors, 43–45, 73
adulthood, 26, 37, 42, 44, 51, 64,
    113, 124
aesthetic perception, 26, 46, 56–60,
    115. See also sensory perception
aesthetic properties, 56–57
aesthetics: childhood connections,
    12; defined, 17; ethics and, 49–50,
    72–73, 83–86, 119; evolutionary
    conception, 8–9; intangible
    aspects of art, 16–17; nonaesthetic
    and aesthetic properties, 56; as
    science of all arts, 17
Aesthetics: Lectures on Fine Art (Hegel),
    16
aesthetics of taste, 74–75, 91, 96; as
    experience and relationship, xiv,
    1–3, 12, 33–34, 43, 46–48, 107,
    110–11, 119–20, 124; ingesting,
    assimilating, and metabolizing, 25;
    marginality of, 7–8. See also taste
affordances, 10, 93

Agamben, Giorgio, 12, 65, 126
"The Age of the World Picture"
    (Heidegger), 68
aisthesis, 7, 93
Alinea (restaurant), 39
analytical exploration, 75
animal attitude, 90–91
animality and humanity, 41–42
"Answering the Question: What Is
    Enlightenment?" (Kant), 124
anthropocentric doctrine of taste,
    90–91
anthropological writings, 62–64, 71
anthropophagy, 71
"antigastronomic" relation, 105–6
Archestratus of Gela, 48, 121
architecture, 74
Aristotelian thought, xiii
art, 15–16; philosophy of, 15, 20–21
Art as Experience (Dewey), 2
art of living, 123
artifacts, 9, 55; creation of, 24–25;
    wine as, 44–45, 109
Athenaeus, 48, 121
atmospheric indifference, 101–6
autobiographical impulse, 5

Babette's Feast, 51

Barbery, Muriel, 34, 81–83

The Baron in the Trees (Calvino), 72

Barthes, Roland, 26, 68, 109, 118–19

Baudelaire, Charles, 97

Baumgarten, Alexander Gottlieb, 7, 17

beautiful (bellum), 49

beauty, ix, 15, 46, 49

beholder, aesthetics of, 45

beliefs, 84–85

Benjamin, Walter, 24, 68, 74, 96

Berkeley, Bishop, 94

Berry, Wendell, 84, 112

Beuys, Joseph, 49

Blanchot, Maurice, 107

blandness, 110

Blumenthal, Heston, 116

The Body Artist (DeLillo), 97

body/mind dualism, 8, 24–25, 30, 93, 106

bonellum, 49

boundaries, 112–14

brain functions, 27

bread, 92, 108, 122, 126

breastfeeding, 41, 46

Brillat-Savarin, Jean Anthelme, 61–62, 90

Brodsky, Joseph, 49

Calvino, Italo, 61–73; *The Baron in the Trees,* 72; *Under the Jaguar Sun,* 62–73, 100, 110; *Sapore Sapere,* 61; "Theft in a Pastry Shop," 101–2

cannibalism, 71

capitalism, aesthetic, 40

The Character of Rain (Nothomb), 31–32, 33, 34–36, 38–39, 90

chefs, 23–24, 65, 73–74

chemical senses, 5

chemico-physical stimuli, 4–5

childhood, 39, 40–42, 85

"childish" dishes, 73–74

Chinese thought, 110, 125–26, 128

Chiva, Matty, 41

chocolate, 31, 33–34, 62

Choke (Palahniuk), 105–6

cocktail party effect, 103

Combal Zero (restaurant), 116

commercial manipulation, 42, 76, 85–86

common good, 132

common sense, viii, 88, 123

communities of affiliation, 55

complete sensation, 62

compulsive indifference, 101–6

conatus, 32

conferences, vii, 27

conflicts, 70–74

consciousness, ix, 116–17

Consumption Exclusion Thesis (Monroe), 19

context, 10, 39–40, 45, 72–73

contingent indifference, 97–101

conviviality, vii, 129, 131–32

cooking, 9, 14–15, 18, 20; gender and, 65, 108; ordinary, 24–25

Critical Reflections on Poetry, Painting and Music (Dubos), 45

criticism, 18–21, 55, 74–83, 129; degeneration in, 80–81

Critique of the Power of Judgment (Kant), 70–71

cultivation of taste, 54–60, 74–75, 82

cultural studies, 61

culture: conflicts and taste, 70–74; food as, 28–29; immaterial, 93–94; nature in, 43–48; semiotics of, 64; taste as, viii, x, 66–67

curiosity, 75–77

Darwin, Charles, 42
defensive strategies, 79
The Deipnosophists (Athenaeus), 48, 121
Deleuze, Gilles, 8
DeLillo, Don, 97, 104
dematerialization, 30
democratization of taste, 83
Democritus, 121
Derrida, Jacques, 1, 4, 70–71
Descartes, René, 15
Dewey, John, 1, 16, 78, 96, 120, 123
Diamond, Cora, 50
dichotomies, vii–viii, xiii, 8, 43, 54, 91
diet, 86–88, 118
dietetics, 86–87
digital data, 80
digital democracy, 83
diplomacy, everyday, 132, 133
direct sensation, 62
disgust, 71–72
distal senses, xiii, 15–16, 25, 32, 107. *See also* hearing; vision
distraction, 74, 96–98, 101–5, 109
Dizionario dei sinonimi (Tommaseo), 61
Documenta exhibition, 21
Dostoyevsky, Fyodor, 49
dressed taste, 26, 44, 47, 51–54, 62–63, 115; image and

representation, 66–70; risk, 78–81. *See also* knowledge
Dubos, Jean-Baptiste, 45–46
duration, 114
duty, 84

ecological paradigm, xi, 1–3, 9, 119, 124–25; indifference and, 89, 91, 93, 96, 103, 108–11, 114; knowledge and, 59–60, 73; pleasure and, 22, 24, 29–30, 32–34, 43
education, aesthetic, 57–58, 84–85, 120
egodicea, 4
elevation strategies, 93
embodied knowledge, 25
emotion, 27–28, 32, 100, 116–17, 134
empathy, 132, 133
encounters, aesthetic, 3
Encyclopédie ou Dictionnaire raisonné des sciences, des arts et des métiers, 22
energy of pleasure, 32, 34
enjoyment, 6, 10, 12, 29–31; indifference and, 105–6, 111, 114; intellectual, 14–15, 54, 80; pleasure and, 43–48; wisdom of taste and, 117, 121
environmental continuum, 9
Epicurean, as term, 48, 121
Epicurus, 3, 16, 27, 48–49, 51, 120–23; "Letter to Menoeceus," 121–22
Erfahrung (experience), 8, 119–20
Erlebnis (experience), 8, 119–20
Eros/Thanatos, 66
essay, 118

ethical appropriateness, 84–85
ethical imagination, 50
ethics, xi–xii, 18–19; aesthetics
    and, 49–50, 72–73, 83–86, 119;
    appreciation of food, 83–86;
    of guest, 128–29; of pleasure,
    48–52
everyday life, x, 2–3, 103
evolutionary approaches, 11, 16–17,
    22
excess food intake, 113–14
exclusivism. *See* taste exclusivism
exigo (to weigh, to examine, to
    assay), 118
exoticism, 73
expectations, 117, 133–34
experience, xiv, 8, 96, 116–20;
    aesthetics of taste and, xiv, 1–3,
    12, 33–34, 43, 46–48, 107, 110–
    11, 119–20, 124; haptic, 65–68,
    75, 109, 114; temporal, 112–14
expertise, ix, ix–x, 34, 76–77, 119;
    wise, 120–24
exploration, 54, 60–61, 70
*The Expression of the Emotions in Man and
    Animals* (Darwin), 42

facial expression, 2, 40–42, 56
fairness, 84
family meal, 72
fasting, 90
The Fat Duck, 116
Feuerbach, Ludwig, 50, 92–93
first contact with food, 11
"The Five Senses" (Serres), 70
Flandrin, Jean-Louis, xiv, 87
flavors, 5
flexibility, 128–30

food: as Culture, viii, x; culture as,
    viii, x; excluded from philosophy,
    16, 19–21, 46, 94–95; nutritional
    and energy-providing function,
    74–75; visual cuisine and cooks,
    67–68
food cultures, 93–94
food production, 22–23
food studies, 14
foodism, 80
Foucault, Michel, 123
Fourier, Charles, 50, 51
Fraser, John Foster, 60
friends, 128, 131
function of food, 74
function of taste, 37, 74

gastronomes, 9, 20–21, 23, 61–62,
    77, 80–81, 90
gastronomy: early modern period,
    87; expertise, ix–x; origin
    of term, 48; as process of
    theoretical existence, 4
Gastronomy (Archestratus of Gela),
    121
gender, 65–66, 71, 107–8
generation gap, 34
Gibson, James, 5, 10, 16
globalization, 74
God, as gustative relationship,
    33–34
good, x–xii; does us "good," 48–52
"good taste," 40, 44
Gourmet Rhapsody (Barbery), 34
gradualist position, 8–9
grammar of taste, 55–56, 85, 108,
    113
grammar of thought, 7

grammar of values, xi
La grande bouffe, 66
grandparents, 35
gratification, delayed, 29–30
guest, ethics of, 128–29
guilt, 2

haptic experiences, 65–68, 75, 109, 114
Harris, Marvin, 72
health, 37–38, 87–88
hearing, 15–16, 67
hedonic drives, 28, 33, 35, 39, 42, 102
Hegel, G. W. F., 16, 18
Heidegger, Martin, 68
hierarchies: animal vs. human, 90–91; cuisine and ordinary cooking, 24–25; gender and food, 65, 107–8; Kantian, 46; nutrition vs. cuisine, 42; reversing, 48; of senses, vii–viii, 7, 8–9, 15–17, 63–64; skills vs. intellectual abilities, 22; taste vs. nourishment, 93–94
"high" culture, viii
Hillman, James, 49
Hippocratic-Galenic medicine, 86–87
hospes (host or guest), 128–29, 131
hospitality, 126, 128–29
Hume, David, 17, 77–78, 123
hunger, aesthetics of, 96, 102
"A Hunger Artist" (Kafka), 90

The Idiot (Dostoyevsky), 49
Il Sole 24 Ore article, 18–19
image, 34–38; acoustic, 67; knowledge and, 66–70; manifest vs. scientific, 95

immaterial culture, 93–94
impermanence of gustatory pleasures, 19–20
In the Shadow of Young Girls in Flower (Proust), 100–101
incorporation and assimilation of food, viii–x, xii–xiii, 1, 3, 6, 14, 17, 68, 79, 125, 134–35; indifference and, 92, 102, 104, 106; knowledge and, 55, 63–64, 67–72; as naked pleasure, 25–26, 29; vital and metabolic aspects, appreciation of, 75
indifference, xv, 7, 12–13, 25–26, 88, 115–16; as aesthetic experience, 102–3; appropriateness of, 91–92, 99–101; chronic, 91; compulsive and atmospheric, 101–6; contingent, 97–101; eating not related to perception, 94–96; extension of pleasure and limits of gustatory exclusivism, 111–14; as history, 96; during intense emotional states, 100; mass production and, 22–23; more open gastronomy and, 91; neutrality, 106–11; pleasure around food, 111–12; theoretical framework, 93–96; water, 108–9
individual pleasure, 46, 59
infants, taste perception, 41
inferior senses, 7, 15
Ingold, Tim, 9, 20, 24
ingredients, 92
intellect, privileging of, 7, 14–15, 24–25
introjection, 63

Irigaray, Luce, 107–8
irony, 134
The Irresistible Inheritance of Wilberforce (Torday), 78–79

judgment of taste, 16, 21, 45–46, 70–71
Jullien, François, 110, 125, 128
justification of pleasure, 10, 27, 39, 47–48

Kafka, Franz, 90
Kant, Immanuel, ix, 16, 18, 30, 46, 70–71; "Answering the Question: What Is Enlightenment?," 124
knowledge, viii, 11–12, 25–26, 53–88, 112, 115; embodied, 25; image and, 66–70; intention and, 26, 43–44, 61, 92, 96, 102; interaction and negotiation, 55, 57; pleasure and, 28, 65; of production, 77–78; taste as embodied, 70; understanding over time, 53–54; values and, 55–56; of the world, 64. *See also* dressed taste
Korsmeyer, Carolyn, 7, 14

language, 31–32, 65–67, 107, 118
Laozi (sage), 108
"L'arte della digestion" (Savater), 18
Latin language, 49
Le Breton, David, 64
Le doux et l'amer (Chiva), 41
Lehre der Nahrungsmittel für das Volk (Moleschott), 92
"Letter to Menoeceus" (Epicurus), 121–22

Lévinas, Emmanuel, 32, 50, 92, 107
Lévi-Strauss, Claude, x, 72
The Life of Hunger (Nothomb), 33–34, 40
Like a Kid in a Sweetshop (video), 116
long-term relationships, 62–63, 66, 100
lowering strategy, viii, x, 23–24
Lullaby (Palahniuk), 103–5, 106

manifest image, 95
marginality, xiv, 6–8, 25
margins, theory of, 26
marshmallow experiment (Stanford University), 29
Marx, Karl, 121
materiality of food, 6, 94–96
meaning, 2, 7
"Mediterranean diet," 88
Melville, Herman, 71–72
memories, 5, 9, 21, 98–99, 114; activated by pleasure, 32, 116–17
Der Mensch ist, was er isst ("Man is what he eats"), 92
Metamorphoses (Ovid), 128–29
metaphorical eating, vii–viii
milk, 109
mimicry, 37, 41
mind/body dualism, 17, 30
mirror, 36
mirror neurons, 37
Moby Dick (Melville), 71–72
moderation, 17–18, 30, 123
molecules, 95–96
Moleschott, Jacob, 92
Montaigne, Michel de, 3, 4, 17, 113, 115, 119–20, 123

mother/infant relationship, 27, 37, 41, 113
mouth, 65, 69, 70
multimodality, x–xi, 8, 68–69, 74, 82
multisensory perception, 40, 68–69, 73, 119, 123

naked pleasure, x, 10, 12, 26, 29, 115; childhood origins of, 40–42; context, 45; de gustibus non est disputandum, 52, 57, 59; as ecological perception, 32; sight and, 40; threefold relational frame, 36–37; as tool of resistance, 51–52. *See also* pleasure
narcissism, 36
narrative, 6
nature: in culture, 43–48; as prereflexive ingenuity, 51; taste not opposed to, 9
necessity, x–xi
negative pleasure, 10
negative taste, 117
neglect of taste, 7
neutrality, 106–11, 118–19
Nietzsche, Friedrich, 50
nociception, 37–38, 74
nonaesthetic properties, 56–57, 59
Nothomb, Amélie, 30–32, 33–36, 38–40, 48, 64, 90, 99, 102
nutrition, 91–92
nutritionism, 91–92, 95, 106, 111

objectivity, viii–ix, xi, xiii
"Of the Standard of Taste" (Hume), 78

On the Aesthetic Education of Man (Schiller), 120
Onfray, Michel, 24
organic and biodynamic food and wine, 85–86
organs of perception, 5
orthorexia, 81, 88
Ovid, 128–29

Palahniuk, Chuck, 103–6
passion, 134
pathology, 38, 40
perception, 5, 7, 16; aesthetic, 26, 46, 56–60, 115; exploration, 54, 60–61, 70; indifference and, 102–3; multisensory, 40, 68–69, 73, 119, 123; sensory, 40, 58–60, 109, 119; two levels of, 59; viewpoint of perceiver, 117
perceptual systems, 5, 16, 40, 73
Phaedo (Plato), 14–15
Philemon and Baucis, 128–29
philosophy, food excluded from, 16, 19–21, 46, 94–95
philosophy of art, 15, 20–21
philosophy with food, 3, 5, 26
phronesis, 118, 123, 126, 128, 133
physical appearance, 106
The Physiology of Taste (Brillat-Savarin), 90
Pierangelini, Fulvio, 41
Plato, 1, 14–15, 16, 18
pleasure, 11, 27–52, 115; adult, 43–44; around food, 111–12; available to all, 45–46; context, 40; denial of, 34–35, 38; ecological paradigm, 22, 24, 29–30, 32–34, 43; emancipative,

pleasure (*continued*)
39, 50; energy of, 32, 34; ethics
of, 48–52; extension of, 111–
14; as first relationship with
food, 25–26; image and, 34–38;
individual, 46, 59; intensity of
appetite and, 43; knowledge
and, 28, 65; memories activated
by, 32; as nature in culture,
43–48; necessary, 7, 16, 25, 30,
46; nutrition and cuisine not
distinct, 43; relationship as
source of, 32; social and cultural
matrix, 39, 42; subordination of,
28; wisdom and, 121–22, 126. *See
also* naked pleasure
"The Pleasures of Eating" (Berry),
84
pop culture, 82–83
pragmatism, 11
preparation, art of, 62–63
preparers of food, 132
privation, morals of, 38–39
production, 77–78, 111–12
protoaesthetics, 91
Proust, Marcel, 21, 30, 98–101
public, 45, 55, 82

quality, ix, 6, 52, 54–60, 121–22,
129

Ratatouille (movie), 81–83
recognition, 5, 71
recurring cycle, 43
reflective sensation, 62
regenerative potential of taste, 51,
69–70
regulation without rules, 124–27

relationship, gustatory, 6, 21, 125;
aesthetics of taste and, xiv, 1–3,
12, 43, 46–48, 107, 110–11,
119–20, 124; "antigastronomic"
relation, 105–6; God as
gustative relationship, 33–34; as
threefold, 36–37
religious dietary laws, 84
representation, 66–70
reproducibility, 68
resistance, 51, 71, 72, 124, 127
Revel, Jacques, 65
"rising strategy," viii
risk, 78–81
Round the World on a Wheel (Fraser), 60
Russell, Bertrand, 53, 75–76, 112

sacrificial cuisine, 71
sage, 118, 125–26
Salernitan School of Medicine, 124
salience, 103
sapio (to know, to have taste), 118
Sapore Sapere (Calvino), 61
Savater, Fernando, 18
savoir-faire, 115
Scabin, David, 116–17
Schiller, Friedrich, 120
scientific image, 95
seductive ability, 56, 57
Sellars, Wilfrid, 95
semiotics of culture, 64
Sennett, Richard, 20, 132
sensation, 5, 7, 62
senses, hierarchy of, vii–viii, 7, 8–9,
15–16
sensitivity, 7, 46, 77, 84, 90, 109,
124; cultural, 23; wisdom of taste
and, 120, 123

sensory perception, 40, 58–60, 109, 119. *See also* aesthetic perception

sensus communis, 51

Serres, Michel, 70

Shusterman, Richard, 119

singularities, 8, 14

situation, 1, 6

smell, 5, 15

social markers, foods as, 73, 77

solitude, 112–13, 131–32

somaesthetics of taste, 119

specificity, 29, 34

Spinoza, Baruch, 15

standard perception, 59

stimulus, 5

The Stranger Next Door (Nothomb), 38

subjective/objective paradigm, viii–ix, xi, 8, 24, 59

sustainability, 83–86

Swann's Way (Proust), 98–101

tactile senses, xiii, 15; cognitive status, 15; haptic experience of food, 65–68, 75, 109, 114

taste: communication of, 25; complexity of, x, xi, 5; cultivation of, 54–60, 74–75, 82; as culture, viii, x, 66–67; as double ability, 61; as embodied knowledge, 25; function of, 37, 74; gender connotation, 66; "good," 40, 44; grammar of, 55–56, 85, 108, 113; from inside, viii, 54, 93, 117–19, 126; judgment of, 16, 21, 45–46, 70–71; as multimodal, x–xi, 8; as multisensory, 68–69,

73; regenerative potential, 51, 69–70; as revolutionary, xiii–xiv; rules for, 9–10; semantic shift, 23; as social construct, 39; social nature of, 112–13; structures of, xiv; system of values, 55–56; temporal experience of, 112–14; three modes of access, 9–10, 25–26, 62, 115–16, 118; visual perception of, 67–69, 75, 113; Western view, 4–5, 15; of wisdom, 118–19; of the world, 64. *See also* aesthetics of taste; dressed taste; wisdom of taste

taste exclusivism, 112–14

taste of nothing, 97

tastelessness, 110

tasting, vs. taste, 1

technical tasting skills, 9

technological development, 22–23

television and cinema, 67–68

Telfer, Elizabeth, 14

temporal experience of taste, 112–14

"Theft in a Pastry Shop" (Calvino), 101–2

theoretical issues, 7, 14

Theory of the Four Movements and the General Destinies (Fourier), 50

to belong to the forest and to the coast, 128, 130

To Speak Is Never Neutral (Irigaray), 107–8

Tommaseo, Niccolò, 61

tongue, 90, 118

Torday, Paul, 78–79

tourism, 60–66

tradition, 73

transitional thought, 125–26, 128
translation, 68
travel, 119
triangulation of perceiver, perceived,
    and environment, xi, 66–67

Under the Jaguar Sun (Calvino),
    62–73, 100, 110
UNESCO 2010, 94
universal appreciation, 44–46

value, 6, 55–56, 83, 92
vegetarianism, 85
virtualization of taste, 68–69
vision, 6–7, 15–16, 40–41;
    nonintentional childhood
    look, 43; television and cinema,
    67–68
visual perception of taste, 67–69,
    75, 113
vitalism, 120
vomit, 71

water, 108–9
wine: adult and cultural terms,
    44–45, 47, 73; as artifact, 44–45,
    109
wine tasting, 54–56, 113; language
    of, 56, 58–59, 130
wisdom, 3, 115; Epicurus on,
    121–22; everyday diplomacy,
    132, 133; expertise and, 120–
    24; hospitality and, 128–29;
    neutrality and, 118–19; origin of
    term, 118; pleasure and, 121–22,
    126; sage, 118, 125–26; taste of,
    118–19
wisdom of taste, 26, 119–20; advice,
    132–35; regulation without rules,
    124–27
Wittgenstein, Ludwig, 26, 49, 80
"The Work of Art in the Age of
    Mechanical Reproduction"
    (Benjamin), 24
World Heritage status, 94

Salt: Grain of Life, Pierre Laszlo, translated by Mary Beth Mader

Culture of the Fork, Giovanni Rebora, translated by Albert Sonnenfeld

French Gastronomy: The History and Geography of a Passion, Jean-Robert Pitte,
translated by Jody Gladding

Pasta: The Story of a Universal Food, Silvano Serventi and Françoise Sabban,
translated by Antony Shugar

Slow Food: The Case for Taste, Carlo Petrini, translated by William McCuaig

Italian Cuisine: A Cultural History, Alberto Capatti and Massimo Montanari,
translated by Áine O'Healy

British Food: An Extraordinary Thousand Years of History, Colin Spencer

A Revolution in Eating: How the Quest for Food Shaped America, James E. McWilliams

Sacred Cow, Mad Cow: A History of Food Fears, Madeleine Ferrières,
translated by Jody Gladding

Molecular Gastronomy: Exploring the Science of Flavor, Hervé This,
translated by M. B. DeBevoise

Food Is Culture, Massimo Montanari, translated by Albert Sonnenfeld

Kitchen Mysteries: Revealing the Science of Cooking, Hervé This,
translated by Jody Gladding

Hog and Hominy: Soul Food from Africa to America, Frederick Douglass Opie

Gastropolis: Food and New York City, edited by Annie Hauck-Lawson
and Jonathan Deutsch

Building a Meal: From Molecular Gastronomy to Culinary Constructivism, Hervé This,
translated by M. B. DeBevoise

Eating History: Thirty Turning Points in the Making of American Cuisine,
Andrew F. Smith

The Science of the Oven, Hervé This, translated by Jody Gladding

Pomodoro! A History of the Tomato in Italy, David Gentilcore

Cheese, Pears, and History in a Proverb, Massimo Montanari, translated
by Beth Archer Brombert

Food and Faith in Christian Culture, edited by Ken Albala and Trudy Eden

The Kitchen as Laboratory: Reflections on the Science of Food and Cooking,
edited by César Vega, Job Ubbink, and Erik van der Linden

Creamy and Crunchy: An Informal History of Peanut Butter, the All-American Food,
Jon Krampner

Let the Meatballs Rest: And Other Stories About Food and Culture, Massimo Montanari,
translated by Beth Archer Brombert

The Secret Financial Life of Food: From Commodities Markets to Supermarkets,
Kara Newman

Drinking History: Fifteen Turning Points in the Making of American Beverages,
Andrew F. Smith

Italian Identity in the Kitchen, or Food and the Nation, Massimo Montanari,
translated by Beth Archer Brombert

Fashioning Appetite: Restaurants and the Making of Modern Identity,
Joanne Finkelstein

The Land of the Five Flavors: A Cultural History of Chinese Cuisine,
Thomas O. Höllmann, translated by Karen Margolis

The Insect Cookbook: Food for a Sustainable Planet, Arnold van Huis, Henk van Gurp,
and Marcel Dicke, translated by Françoise Takken-Kaminker
and Diane Blumenfeld-Schaap

Religion, Food, and Eating in North America, edited by Benjamin E. Zeller,
Marie W. Dallam, Reid L. Neilson, and Nora L. Rubel

Umami: Unlocking the Secrets of the Fifth Taste, Ole G. Mouritsen
and Klavs Styrbæk, translated by Mariela Johansen
and designed by Jonas Drotner Mouritsen

The Winemaker's Hand: Conversations on Talent, Technique, and Terroir,
Natalie Berkowitz

Chop Suey, USA: The Story of Chinese Food in America, Yong Chen

Note-by-Note Cooking: The Future of Food, Hervé This,
translated by M. B. DeBevoise

Medieval Flavors: Food, Cooking, and the Table, Massimo Montanari,
translated by Beth Archer Brombert

Another Person's Poison: A History of Food Allergy, Matthew Smith

Milton Keynes UK
Ingram Content Group UK Ltd.
UKHW041046150824
446776UK00002BA/2/J